EASY RECIPES & RECOMMENDATIONS
During & After Treatment

EATING WELL

Through Cancer

HOLLY CLEGG & GERALD MILETELLO, M.D.

Also by Holly Clegg

The Holly Clegg Trim & Terrific™ Cookbook: More than 500 Fast, Easy, and Healthy Recipes
Holly Clegg Trim & Terrific™ Home Entertaining The Easy Way

Nutritional Analysis by
Tammi Hancock, RD

Cover Design by
Danielle Chapman

LCCCN: 2001116006

ISBN: 0-9610888-7-7

First Printing	10,000 copies	April 2001
Second Printing	15,000 copies	November 2001
Third Printing	7,500 copies	May 2003
Fourth Printing	7,500 copies	March 2004
Fifth Printing	7,000 copies	September 2004
Sixth Printing	25,000 copies	February 2005
Seventh Printing	20,000 copies	October 2005

Printed in Korea

TABLE OF CONTENTS

DEDICATION

**This book is dedicated to Holly's father, Jerry Berkowitz,
and everyone whose life has been touched by cancer.**

Holly's Note

I enjoy eating and as author of the *"Trim & Terrific"* cookbook series, I strive to create recipes that are easy, healthy and delicious. Dr. Gerald Miletello, an oncologist, provided the motivation for this book. Because of my love of food, this is an opportunity for me to use my expertise in recipe development to create appropriate and best tolerated food addressing the side effects of cancer treatment. PEOPLE WITH CANCER STILL NEED TO EAT! I started researching nutrition and diet for cancer patients and found the information available to be very technical, made claims or insisted on a radical new style of eating patterns.

I believe a person should not have to eat food that does not taste good. My "no sacrifice of taste" philosophy throughout my *"Trim & Terrific"* cookbooks is my approach once again in creating tasty, healthy, and easy recipes. My challenge was to provide appealing recipes that ease side effects during treatment. Good nutrition and eating is essential to staying healthy and having the necessary energy.

Working with Dr. Miletello provided me with an understanding of what happens to a person having treatment. With this in mind, I tried to focus on quick recipes and include foods labeled as the "super foods" helpful in fighting cancer: cruciferous vegetables, yogurt instead of sour cream, beans, fruits, garlic, beta-carotene rich foods, fiber rich foods, beans, and fish. The recipes I created are familiar and include favorite foods but with an awareness of what a person can eat at each stage of treatment.

The *Caregiver* chapter is helpful for caregivers, family and friends. After treatment, hopefully, the joy of eating will return and the *Healthy Eating Post Treatment* chapter has recipes for a long term healthier lifestyle. *Menus* provide complete meal ideas appropriate at that time. As many recipes overlap from chapter to chapter, I think the *Recipe Cross Reference List* will prove to be a popular and invaluable source of reference.

Each recipe includes the nutritional analysis and diabetic exchange. Optional ingredients are not included in the analysis and it is based on the smaller portion serving. *Doc's Note* and my tidbits provide each recipe with valuable information. As I tested these recipes on my family, I must emphasize that anyone who enjoys a healthier approach to cooking, with or without a health problem, will also enjoy this book.

As I began my work on this cookbook, unexpectedly, it became very personal. My father was diagnosed with larynx cancer and had to undergo treatment. Eating is a necessity and I hope these recipes will make treatment a little easier with the comfort of food. My father and I love eating, and I know he will enjoy the *Healthy Eating Post Treatment* chapter for many years to come as you or your friends will! Cancer has touched everyone's life in some way and at some time, and Gerald Miletello and I hope our book will touch you.

Holly Berkowitz Clegg

Dr. Miletello's Note

Cancer is an uncontrolled growth of cells that destroys the function of normal cells. Cancer can involve one organ of the body or every organ, including the blood. Once your treatment for cancer begins, you will likely notice a change in your appetite and your senses of taste and smell. The changes are secondary to normal cells being destroyed, as well as cancer cells. The goal of cancer treatment is to destroy the cancer cells and allow the good cells to flourish.

The loss of appetite, called anorexia, is one of the most common side-effects of chemotherapy. Anorexia can also result from radiation therapy, stress, anxiety, depression, and cancer itself. Trying to maintain adequate calorie intake during this time can be very difficult for the patient or caregiver who is trying to prepare food.

You have to maintain your nutrition in order to maintain your health and strength to enable you to fight the cancer. Certain foods that you once loved may no longer appeal to you. Your taste and cravings may change from day to day and hour to hour. You may develop a sore mouth and tongue or you may have trouble swallowing. Fortunately, these side-effects only last three to eight days following chemotherapy. Diarrhea and/or constipation may occur at any time during your treatments. If you are taking narcotics, constipation can become a significant problem.

Diarrhea is a condition marked by abnormally frequent bowel movements that are softer than usual. Cramping may accompany diarrhea. Diarrhea may be secondary to chemotherapy, radiation or surgery to the bowel or sometimes secondary to bowel infections from antibiotics. Milk intolerance is also a cause of diarrhea.

Neutropenia, low white blood cell count, follows most chemotherapy treatments at some time. Neutropenia normally lasts for 3–7 days. I recommend avoiding fresh fruits, vegetables, raw meat, or fish during the time your blood counts are low. As soon as your counts have returned to normal, you can return to a regular diet.

The lining or mucosa of the gastrointestinal tract, which includes the inside of the mouth and throat, is one of the most sensitive areas of the body. Many chemotherapy drugs can inflame the lining of the mouth. Many drugs can also cause ulcerations or sores to develop. This can cause difficulty maintaining your nutrition.

We hope that we can offer suggestions for food and drinks that will appeal to you, as well as suggestions for foods that will assist in managing some of the side-effects of chemotherapy. We have also included helpful hints for family and caregivers. Our last section involves healthy eating post treatment.

Although no diet has been proven to prevent cancer, health authorities agree that a properly chosen diet can reduce the risk of developing certain cancers. We also feel that a properly chosen diet can help you to fight cancer once you have developed it.

Note that any of the recipes can be tried at any time during your treatment. These recipes are all low in fat and healthy. We have also included high calorie versions of some of the recipes for whenever needed. Also, note that these foods are for everyone, not only the cancer patient. The entire family can enjoy each and every one of these dishes. We have also included diabetic exchanges since some patients are diabetic and some of the drugs we use to treat cancer will elevate your blood sugar.

Gerald Miletello, M.D.

RECIPE CROSS REFERENCE LIST

	Day of Chemotherapy	Neutropenia	Diarrhea	Constipation	Sore Mouth	Snacks	Caregiver	Post Treatment Healthy Eating
All Natural Laxative, p. 122				✓				
Almost Better Than Sex Cake, p. 237	✓	✓			✓	✓	✓	✓
Ambrosia Crumble, p. 242				✓		✓	✓	✓
Apple Lasagna, p. 27	✓	✓		✓	✓	✓	✓	✓
Applesauce Oatmeal, p. 138	✓	✓		✓	✓	✓	✓	✓
Artichoke Soup, p. 62	✓				✓	✓	✓	✓
Artichoke Squares, p. 160		✓				✓	✓	✓
Asparagus and Brie Pizza, p. 164						✓	✓	✓
Asparagus and Potato Soup, p. 33	✓				✓	✓	✓	✓
Avocado Soup, p. 140	✓			✓	✓	✓	✓	✓
Awesome Milk Shake, p. 150	✓	✓			✓	✓	✓	✓
Baked Acorn Squash, p. 141	✓	✓		✓	✓	✓	✓	✓
Baked Beans, p. 112				✓		✓	✓	✓
Baked Corn Casserole, p. 113		✓		✓		✓	✓	✓
Baked Fish, p. 47	✓					✓	✓	✓
Baked French Toast, p. 26	✓	✓	✓		✓	✓	✓	✓
Baked Peach Delight, p. 73	✓	✓				✓	✓	✓
Baked Topped Fish, p. 226	✓	✓	✓		✓	✓	✓	✓
Banana Bran Muffins, p. 126				✓		✓	✓	✓
Banana Bread, p. 174	✓		✓		✓	✓	✓	✓
Banana Cake with Cream Cheese Icing, p. 238						✓	✓	✓
Banana Pudding, p. 89	✓		✓		✓	✓	✓	✓
Banana Pudding Trifle, p. 52	✓				✓	✓	✓	✓
Banana Puff, p. 81	✓	✓	✓		✓	✓	✓	✓
Basic Broccoli, p. 113				✓		✓	✓	✓
Basic Weight Gain Shake, p. 75	✓	✓			✓	✓	✓	✓
Beefy Vegetable Soup, p. 203				✓		✓	✓	✓

	Day of Chemotherapy	Neutropenia	Diarrhea	Constipation	Sore Mouth	Snacks	Caregiver	Post Treatment Healthy Eating
Berry French Toast, p. 25	✓			✓	✓	✓	✓	✓
Black and White Bean Salad, p. 110				✓		✓	✓	✓
Black Bean and Corn Salad, p. 111				✓		✓	✓	✓
Blueberry Pancakes, p. 24	✓					✓	✓	✓
Bread Pudding Florentine, p. 28	✓	✓		✓	✓	✓	✓	✓
Breakfast Casserole, p. 176						✓	✓	✓
Broiled Shrimp, p. 48	✓					✓	✓	✓
Caesar Salad, p. 208						✓	✓	✓
Cantaloupe Banana Smoothie, p. 139	✓			✓	✓	✓	✓	✓
Carrot Soufflé, p. 143	✓	✓		✓	✓	✓	✓	✓
Cauliflower Soup, p. 177	✓	✓			✓	✓	✓	✓
Cauliflower Supreme, p. 215				✓		✓	✓	✓
Cereal Mixture, p. 153	✓			✓		✓	✓	✓
Cheese Broccoli Soup, p. 60		✓			✓	✓	✓	✓
Cheese Quesadillas, p. 166	✓	✓			✓	✓	✓	✓
Cheesy Macaroni, p. 41	✓	✓			✓	✓	✓	✓
Cheesy Shrimp-Rice Casserole, p. 66	✓	✓			✓	✓	✓	✓
Chess Pie, p. 50	✓	✓			✓	✓	✓	✓
Chicken and Black Bean Enchiladas, p. 186				✓		✓	✓	✓
Chicken, Barley, and Bow-Tie Soup, p. 35	✓			✓		✓	✓	✓
Chicken Diane with Wild Rice, p. 44	✓					✓	✓	✓
Chicken Piccata, p. 68	✓	✓				✓	✓	✓
Chicken Pot Pie, p. 67		✓				✓	✓	✓
Chicken Primavera, p. 223				✓		✓	✓	✓
Chicken Salad, p. 106				✓		✓	✓	✓
Chicken Scampi, p. 87		✓	✓			✓	✓	✓
Chicken Soup, p. 34	✓					✓	✓	✓
Chicken Tortilla Soup, p. 180				✓		✓	✓	✓
Chicken with Bean Sauce, p. 221				✓		✓	✓	✓

	Day of Chemotherapy	Neutropenia	Diarrhea	Constipation	Sore Mouth	Snacks	Caregiver	Post Treatment Healthy Eating
Chocolate Layered Dessert, p. 193						✓	✓	✓
Cinnamon Quick Bread, p. 156	✓	✓			✓	✓	✓	✓
Cinnamon Rolls, p. 23	✓	✓	✓			✓	✓	✓
Coffee Cake, p. 169	✓	✓				✓	✓	✓
Company Chicken, p. 184						✓	✓	✓
Cornmeal Fruity Snack Muffins, p. 155	✓			✓		✓	✓	✓
Couscous Salad, p. 204				✓		✓	✓	✓
Crabmeat Egg Casserole, p. 31	✓					✓	✓	✓
Cranberry Yam Bread, p. 129	✓	✓		✓		✓	✓	✓
Cream Cheese Bread Pudding, p. 148	✓	✓			✓	✓	✓	✓
Cream of Spinach and Brie Soup, p. 202					✓	✓	✓	✓
Cream of Spinach Soup, p. 179				✓	✓	✓	✓	✓
Creamed Double Potatoes, p. 144				✓	✓	✓	✓	✓
Creamy Squash Casserole, p. 82		✓	✓			✓	✓	✓
Curried Rice and Sweet Potatoes, p. 213				✓		✓	✓	✓
Easy Banana Bread, p. 80	✓	✓	✓		✓	✓	✓	✓
Easy Broccoli Potato Bake, p. 214				✓		✓	✓	✓
Easy Crab Soup, p. 63		✓				✓	✓	✓
Egg Noodle Casserole, p. 30	✓	✓			✓	✓	✓	✓
Egg Soufflé, p. 29	✓				✓	✓	✓	✓
Eggplant Parmesan, p. 219				✓		✓	✓	✓
Fresh Fruit Dip, p. 158	✓					✓	✓	✓
Fresh Tomato and Cheese Pizza, p. 163						✓	✓	✓
Fried Rice Stir-Fry, p. 212				✓		✓	✓	✓
Fruity Couscous Salad, p. 36	✓			✓		✓	✓	✓
German Chocolate Angel Pie, p. 147	✓	✓			✓	✓	✓	✓
Glazed Bananas, p. 90	✓		✓			✓	✓	✓
Granola, p. 94				✓		✓	✓	✓
Grilled Pork Tenderloin, p. 234			✓			✓	✓	✓

	Day of Chemotherapy	Neutropenia	Diarrhea	Constipation	Sore Mouth	Snacks	Caregiver	Post Treatment Healthy Eating
Ham and Cheese Grits Quiche, p. 145	✓	✓			✓	✓	✓	✓
Heavenly Yam Delight, p. 71		✓				✓	✓	✓
Herb Baked Salmon, p. 229						✓	✓	✓
Herbed Shrimp, p. 224						✓	✓	✓
Honey Bran Prune Muffins, p. 125				✓		✓	✓	✓
Hot Cocoa Drink Supplement, p. 76	✓	✓			✓	✓	✓	✓
Hot Fruit Compote, p. 70	✓	✓		✓	✓	✓	✓	✓
Italian Chicken, p. 45	✓					✓	✓	✓
Italian Pasta Salad, p. 161						✓	✓	✓
Italian Spinach Pie, p. 167				✓		✓	✓	✓
Italian Veal Supreme, p. 236				✓		✓	✓	✓
Italian-Style Pot Roast, p. 233				✓		✓	✓	✓
Jumbo Stuffed Shells, p. 189				✓		✓	✓	✓
Lemon Angel Food Cake, p. 53	✓	✓			✓	✓	✓	✓
Lemon Berry Bread, p. 128	✓			✓		✓	✓	✓
Linguine Florentine, p. 64		✓			✓	✓	✓	✓
Loaded Enchiladas, p. 231				✓		✓	✓	✓
Loaded Potatoes, p. 65	✓	✓			✓	✓	✓	✓
Mandarin Chicken Salad, p. 107				✓		✓	✓	✓
Mango Salad, p. 201	✓					✓	✓	✓
Manicotti, p. 182				✓		✓	✓	✓
Meat Loaf, p. 121				✓		✓	✓	✓
Meaty Cabbage Casserole, p. 232				✓		✓	✓	✓
Melon Soup, p. 136	✓				✓	✓	✓	✓
Mexican Chicken Casserole, p. 185				✓		✓	✓	✓
Minestrone Soup, p. 103				✓		✓	✓	✓
Mini Cheese Pizzas, p. 162	✓	✓				✓	✓	✓
Mocha Cappuccino Pudding Pie, p. 72		✓			✓	✓	✓	✓
Mocha Meringue Mounds, p. 172	✓	✓	✓		✓	✓	✓	✓

	Day of Chemotherapy	Neutropenia	Diarrhea	Constipation	Sore Mouth	Snacks	Caregiver	Post Treatment Healthy Eating
Mock Chocolate Eclair, p. 54	✓	✓			✓	✓	✓	✓
Mushroom Barley Soup, p. 99				✓		✓	✓	✓
No Bake Cookies, p. 170						✓	✓	✓
Noodle Pudding, p. 142		✓			✓	✓	✓	✓
Oatmeal Chocolate Cake, p. 130	✓			✓		✓	✓	✓
Oatmeal Pancakes, p. 200	✓	✓		✓	✓	✓	✓	✓
Orzo Asparagus Toss, p. 42	✓			✓		✓	✓	✓
Oven Fried Parmesan Chicken, p. 85	✓	✓	✓			✓	✓	✓
Paella Salad, p. 205				✓		✓	✓	✓
Pasta Salad, p. 190				✓		✓	✓	✓
Pasta Toss, p. 83			✓			✓	✓	✓
Peach Crumble, p. 131	✓			✓	✓	✓	✓	✓
Peach Smoothie, p. 74	✓	✓			✓	✓	✓	✓
Peach Soup, p. 32	✓					✓	✓	✓
Peach Weight Gain Shake, p. 74	✓	✓			✓	✓	✓	✓
Peanut Butter-Banana Pie, p. 241					✓	✓	✓	✓
Perfect Pasta, p. 39	✓	✓			✓	✓	✓	✓
Pesto Pasta, p. 216						✓	✓	✓
Piña Colada Bundt Cake, p. 195	✓					✓	✓	✓
Pineapple Bread Pudding with Lemon Apricot Sauce, p. 51	✓			✓		✓	✓	✓
Potato Pizza, p. 40	✓					✓	✓	✓
Pretzel Strawberry Gelatin, p. 192	✓					✓	✓	✓
Pumpkin Soup, p. 59	✓	✓			✓	✓	✓	✓
Quick and Easy Corn and Shrimp Soup, p. 178						✓	✓	✓
Quick Cheese Grits, p. 58	✓	✓	✓		✓	✓	✓	✓
Quick Cheesy Potato Soup, p. 183					✓	✓	✓	✓
Quick Chicken and Dumplings, p. 46	✓	✓			✓	✓	✓	✓

	Day of Chemotherapy	Neutropenia	Diarrhea	Constipation	Sore Mouth	Snacks	Caregiver	Post Treatment Healthy Eating
Quick Chicken Pasta, p. 86			✓			✓	✓	✓
Quick Herb Chicken, p. 222	✓		✓			✓	✓	✓
Quick Shrimp Sauté, p. 146					✓	✓	✓	✓
Quick Veggie Soup, p. 100				✓		✓	✓	✓
Raspberry Spinach Salad, p. 209				✓		✓	✓	✓
Red Beans and Rice, p. 119				✓		✓	✓	✓
Rice Taco Salad, p. 181						✓	✓	✓
Roasted Turkey Breast, p. 84	✓	✓	✓			✓	✓	✓
Salmon Patties with Horseradish Caper Sauce, p. 227						✓	✓	✓
Savory Lamb Chops, p. 235						✓	✓	✓
Seafood and Wild Rice Casserole, p. 187				✓		✓	✓	✓
Seven-Layer Salad, p. 206						✓	✓	✓
Shrimp and Squash Scampi, p. 88			✓			✓	✓	✓
Shrimp and Wild Rice Salad, p. 108				✓		✓	✓	✓
Shrimp, Peppers, and Cheese Grits, p. 225						✓	✓	✓
Shrimp Rice Casserole, p. 191						✓	✓	✓
Simple Vichyssoise, p. 136					✓	✓	✓	✓
Simply Delicious Chicken, p. 43	✓					✓	✓	✓
Simply Salmon Pasta, p. 228						✓	✓	✓
Snack Mix, p. 154				✓		✓	✓	✓
Southwestern Chicken with Salsa, p. 220						✓	✓	✓
Southwestern Pasta, p. 120				✓		✓	✓	✓
Southwestern Stuffed Potatoes, p. 168				✓		✓	✓	✓
Spinach and Cheese Tortilla Pizza, p. 165						✓	✓	✓
Spinach Dip, p. 157	✓	✓			✓	✓	✓	✓
Spinach Layered Dish, p. 175	✓			✓		✓	✓	✓
Spinach Rice with Feta, p. 211				✓		✓	✓	✓
Split Pea Soup, p. 101	✓			✓		✓	✓	✓

	Day of Chemotherapy	Neutropenia	Diarrhea	Constipation	Sore Mouth	Snacks	Caregiver	Post Treatment Healthy Eating
Squash and Tomato Casserole, p. 217				✓		✓	✓	✓
Squash Bisque, p. 102				✓		✓	✓	✓
Strawberry Angel Food Cake, p. 240	✓					✓	✓	✓
Strawberry Bread, p. 127	✓			✓		✓	✓	✓
Strawberry Fruit Dip, p. 158	✓					✓	✓	✓
Strawberry Raspberry Soup, p. 95	✓			✓		✓	✓	✓
Strawberry Salsa, p. 159				✓		✓	✓	✓
Strawberry Slush, p. 152				✓				
Strawberry Weight Gain Shake, p. 149	✓			✓		✓	✓	✓
Strawberry Soup, p. 32	✓			✓		✓	✓	✓
Surprise Rolls, p. 22	✓	✓				✓	✓	✓
Sweet and Sour Broccoli Salad, p. 207				✓		✓	✓	✓
Sweet Potato and Apple Soup, p. 104				✓	✓	✓	✓	✓
Sweet Potato, Apple, and Walnut Muffins, p. 124				✓		✓	✓	✓
Sweet Potato Cheesecake, p. 196					✓	✓	✓	✓
Sweet Potato Pancakes with Apple Walnut Topping, p. 96				✓		✓	✓	✓
Sweet Potato Pound Cake, p. 194						✓	✓	✓
Sweet Potato Shake, p. 140				✓	✓	✓	✓	✓
Tasty Brown Rice, p. 114				✓		✓	✓	✓
Tropical Green Salad, p. 210				✓		✓	✓	✓
Tropical Pizza, p. 132				✓		✓	✓	✓
Tropical Salsa, p. 97				✓		✓	✓	✓
Tuna Pasta Salad, p. 109				✓		✓	✓	✓
Tuna Salad, p. 38	✓			✓		✓	✓	✓
Tuna Steaks with Horseradish Sauce, p. 230						✓	✓	✓
Turkey Jambalaya, p. 188				✓		✓	✓	✓

	Day of Chemotherapy	Neutropenia	Diarrhea	Constipation	Sore Mouth	Snacks	Caregiver	Post Treatment Healthy Eating
Two-Potato Bisque, p. 61	✓	✓			✓	✓	✓	✓
Vegetable Lasagna, p. 118				✓		✓	✓	✓
Veggie Angel Hair, p. 116				✓		✓	✓	✓
Very Good Veal, p. 69		✓				✓	✓	✓
Waldorf Pasta Salad, p. 37	✓			✓		✓	✓	✓
Waldorf Salad, p. 105				✓		✓	✓	✓
Watermelon Slush, p. 139	✓				✓	✓	✓	✓
Weight Gain Pancakes, p. 137		✓			✓	✓	✓	✓
White Bean and Tortellini Soup, p. 98				✓		✓	✓	✓
Wild Rice and Barley Pilaf, p. 115				✓		✓	✓	✓
Yam Biscuits, p. 49	✓	✓			✓	✓	✓	✓
Yam Cake with Cranberry Cream Cheese Filling, p. 239				✓		✓	✓	✓
Yam Cornbread Stuffing, p. 218				✓		✓	✓	✓
Yam Veggie Wraps, p. 117				✓		✓	✓	✓
Yummy Cookies, p. 171	✓	✓		✓		✓	✓	✓
Zucchini Oatmeal-Raisin Muffins, p. 123				✓		✓	✓	✓

Notes

DAY OF CHEMOTHERAPY AND FOLLOWING TREATMENT

- *What should I eat prior to my treatment?*
- *Is there a certain time of day that is better for eating?*
- *I only like two foods!*
- *I cannot eat, but I can drink!*
- *Nothing tastes good!*
- *How do I overcome weight loss?*
- *How do I prepare my pantry?*

Not all treatments will cause nausea, vomiting or loss of appetite. The acute side effects, such as nausea, are caused by the destruction of rapidly dividing cells lining the gastrointestinal tract. This is one of the primary causes for the loss of appetite, nausea, vomiting and sore mouth.

I recommend a low fat, light meal prior to your treatment, including foods such as cereal, toast, oatmeal, grits, fruit cocktail, peach or pear nectar. Twenty-four hours following your treatment I would try liquids, soups, puddings or sandwiches. Try to avoid high fat, fried or greasy foods for the first twenty-four to forty-eight hours following treatment. If you find that only two foods appeal to you, then there is nothing wrong with eating those foods until you feel like expanding your diet. Water is essential. I recommend eight to ten glasses of water per day. Supplements such as Boost are excellent choices if you only feel like drinking.

You may experience a sore or dry mouth as well as a total loss of appetite. This may require a little creativity on you part to keep your nutritional status on the positive side. You may find it impossible to eat three large meals per day. This is the first time in your life that someone is going to recommend to you that you eat snacks daily. Six small meals instead of three large meals will increase your caloric intake. Remember hydration is of utmost importance. Keep a glass of liquid available at all times. (Water with a slice of lemon, apple juice, carrot juice, cranberry juice etc.) Do not forget your mouth care protocol. This really will keep your mouth refreshed and decrease ulcer formation.

Mix one teaspoon of salt with one teaspoon of baking soda in a quart of water. Rinse and spit after each meal or at least four times per day. Mix fresh each morning using tap water.

Remember your mouth will get better. The soreness normally clears within a few days. Food is medicine. You have to eat to get through these treatments and back to normal. Rinsing with Ulcerease, Viscous Xylocaine, or Cephacol lozenges may soothe your mouth before a meal. Avoid any food that may irritate your mouth. This would include oranges, lemons, tomato sauces, crackers and alcohol. Avoid hot or extremely cold foods since they tend to irritate your mouth.

Foods at room temperature or slightly cool foods are much more soothing. Try cutting your food into small pieces, cook food until tender or even try pureeing food with a food processor. Drinking with a straw will sometimes help liquids go down easier.

DAY OF CHEMOTHERAPY AND FOLLOWING TREATMENT TIPS

- Eat smaller portions more frequently. Drink fluids between meals instead of with food.
- Eat by the clock at regularly scheduled times. Your appetite signal may not be intact.
- Eat between meals with high-protein diet supplements, milkshakes, puddings, or nutritional energy drink supplement.
- Add cream or butter to soups, cooked cereals, and vegetables to increase calories. Add gravies and sauces to vegetables, meat, poultry and fish until weight loss is no longer a problem.
- Add extra protein to your diet by using fortified milk, peanut butter, cheese and chopped hard boiled eggs.
- Try things to enhance smell, appearance, and texture of food. Be creative with desserts.
- Choose foods you like as long as you do not have dietary restrictions.
- Exercise approximately 30 minutes before meals, to try to stimulate your appetite.
- Try to make mealtimes pleasant by setting an attractive table and by eating with family or friends.
- Plan menus in advance. Have some food frozen and ready to heat and serve.

If you experience changes in your taste, hopefully these suggestions will help:

- ❖ Tart candies, peppermint or lemon drops may reduce the sensations of bitter or sour taste. Try choosing sugarless kinds. Try tart foods such as lemonade.

- ❖ If you experience that "metallic" taste in meat, try marinating meat in a reduced sodium soy sauce or fat free Italian dressing to intensify the flavor. If red meat doesn't work, try eating chicken, seafood or beans for protein.

- ❖ Add extra seasoning or salt but a rule of thumb is to add a little at a time to see if you can perk up those taste buds. Use stronger seasonings such as garlic and onions.

- ❖ Add strongly flavored juices or relishes.

- ❖ The taste of cold foods may not affect your taste buds so try more of them.

- ❖ Try eating foods that don't have strong odors.

- ❖ Eat foods at room temperature.

- ❖ Use plastic utensils if you're bothered by a bitter or metallic taste.

- ❖ Here's a great time to try new foods. Maybe foods that you didn't enjoy in the past will be palate pleasing now.

- ❖ Sucking on a thin slice of dill pickle, prior to meals, will sometimes stimulate your taste buds.

Stocking the Pantry

Preparation and organization are the two key words. The goal of a well stocked pantry should be to have enough food stored to prepare satisfying meals to limit the trips to the grocery store. Be sure to consider, along with the pantry, the refrigerator and freezer.

Begin by including items that you know you like and use most often. Gradually add to your herb and spice inventory. Remember, at this time in your life, your tastes might be slightly different and the pantry may need to include items that appeal to you now. A variety of pasta, rice, and beans and grains may be included, however, if you don't have the exact kind called for in a recipe, just substitute another type you have in the pantry. Canned broths, canned tomatoes, and olive oil are staple items that will be used often.

For the freezer, purchase skinless boneless chicken breasts, pork tenderloins, and ground sirloin. Whenever you are buying meat, always look for the leanest cuts which have a round or sirloin in their name. Then trim any visible fat before preparing. Try making individual hamburger patties wrapped in plastic wrap for a quick pull out. They can be used for sandwiches or defrosted for a recipe. Frozen yogurts are great for that ice cream urge and bags of frozen fruit will be useful. When preparing soups, double the recipe and freeze in zip top bags. Get rid of the air bubbles and they stack easily in the freezer. Convenience items such as frozen veggies are a must and can include spinach, broccoli or your favorites.

For the refrigerator, purchase low fat or fat free dairy products. If you need extra calories, there will be other opportunities as you don't need extra saturated fat. Eggs, margarine, and cheese are also dairy staples.

Tips to Ease At-Home Cooking

- Wash and dry lettuce and seal in plastic containers or a greens bag for easy use.
- Wash, cut up and store veggies to have ready for snacks or use in recipes.
- Raid the salad bar for cut up veggies for recipes or for ready to eat products.
- Shred cheese and store in zip top bags or buy shredded cheese.
- When chopping onion or garlic, chop more than needed and store in zip top bags in the freezer for later use.
- Double recipes to freeze some for a later date or freeze extra.

MENUS

Foods to eat on the day of chemotherapy and following treatment

Morning of Chemotherapy

Eggs - Cereal - Juice
Oatmeal - Grits - Fruit
Tea - Coffee - Sports Drink

Evening of Chemotherapy

Soup - Cheese Toast - Water - Sports Drink
Pudding - Raisins - Noodles with Cheese
Peanut Butter and Jelly Sandwich
Ham and Cheese Sandwich
Remember 6 to 8 cups of fluid per day
Nutritional Supplement Shake

Morning Following Chemotherapy

Tea and Toast
Fresh Fruit
Yogurt
Instant Breakfast

Lunch 24 Hours Post Chemotherapy

Chicken Soup (p. 34)
Mango Salad (p. 201)
Tuna Salad (p. 38)
Water

Dinner 24 Hours Post Chemotherapy

Perfect Pasta (p. 39)
Cheesy Macaroni (p. 41)
Simply Delicious Chicken (p. 43)
Yam Biscuits (p. 49)
Water

SURPRISE ROLLS

*Here's a high carb breakfast to keep
those calories and energy in you.*

3	tablespoons light brown sugar	1	(8-ounce) can reduced-fat crescent dinner rolls
1	teaspoon ground cinnamon	8	large marshmallows
		2	tablespoons margarine, melted

Preheat oven to 375 degrees. Coat 8 muffin cups in a muffin tin with nonstick cooking spray. In a small bowl, mix together the brown sugar and cinnamon; set aside. Separate the dough into triangles and lay flat on a work surface. Dip marshmallows in the melted margarine and roll in the sugar mixture. Wrap one triangle around each marshmallow and pinch the dough together. Place each one in a muffin tin. Drizzle any extra margarine over the top of the rolls in the pan. Bake for 8 to 12 minutes or until done.

Makes 8 rolls

Doc's Notes:

A roll with an apple or banana will get you going. Very light and easy on the stomach.

NUTRITIONAL INFORMATION PER SERVING

Calories	169	Saturated Fat (g)	2
Protein (g)	2	Dietary Fiber (g)	0
Carbohydrate (g)	23	Cholesterol (mg)	0
Fat (g)	7	Sodium (mg)	276
Cal. from Fat (%)	40		

Diabetic Exchanges: 1 starch, 0.5 other carb., 1 fat

CINNAMON ROLLS

*When you have the urge for a wonderful cinnamon roll, make
this quick recipe using canned biscuits and pantry ingredients.*

1 (10-biscuit) can
   refrigerated biscuits or
   whole wheat biscuits
4 tablespoons margarine,
   softened

2 tablespoons sugar
1 teaspoon ground cinnamon
¼ cup raisins, optional
¼ cup chopped pecans,
   optional

Preheat oven to 425 degrees. Flatten each biscuit with your hand or a
rolling pin. Spread each biscuit with margarine. In a small bowl, combine
the sugar and cinnamon together. Sprinkle cinnamon mixture on top
of margarine; sprinkle with raisin and pecans, if desired. Roll up each
biscuit from one side to the other. On an ungreased 15x10x1-inch
baking sheet, arrange each biscuit roll to form a circle touching one
end of the roll to the other. Bake for 8 to 10 minutes.

Makes 10 rolls

Doc's Notes:
Great dessert or breakfast accompaniment.

NUTRITIONAL INFORMATION PER SERVING

Calories 101
Protein (g) 1
Carbohydrate (g) 12
Fat (g) 5
Cal. from Fat (%) 46

Saturated Fat (g) 1
Dietary Fiber (g) 0
Cholesterol (mg) 0
Sodium (mg) 233

Diabetic Exchanges: 1 starch, 1 fat

BLUEBERRY PANCAKES

*These pancakes are so good you won't
need much syrup or margarine.*

1 cup buttermilk	1 teaspoon baking powder
4 large egg whites	½ teaspoon baking soda
2 tablespoons sugar	1 cup blueberries, fresh or
1½ tablespoons canola oil	frozen (thawed)
1 cup all-purpose flour	

In a large mixing bowl, beat together the buttermilk, egg whites, sugar, and oil. In a another mixing bowl, combine together the flour, baking powder, and baking soda. Add the flour mixture to the buttermilk mixture, blending well. Stir the blueberries in gently. Coat a nonstick skillet with nonstick cooking spray and heat over medium-high heat. Pour the batter in ¼-cup portions onto the skillet and cook until brown on both sides and firm to touch, about 3 minutes per side.

Makes 8 to 10 pancakes

Doc's Notes:

You can substitute vanilla nutritional energy drink supplement for the buttermilk. Blueberries are a good source of phyto chemicals which may help prevent cancer.

NUTRITIONAL INFORMATION PER SERVING

Calories	98	Saturated Fat (g)	0
Protein (g)	4	Dietary Fiber (g)	1
Carbohydrate (g)	16	Cholesterol (mg)	1
Fat (g)	2	Sodium (mg)	160
Cal. from Fat (%)	22		

Diabetic Exchanges: 1 starch

BERRY FRENCH TOAST

Use whatever fresh berries you can find or pull them out of the freezer and enjoy this incredible version of French toast. Try using whole grain bread.

5	cups mixed berries (strawberries and blueberries, etc.)		I	large egg
¾	cup sugar plus 1 tablespoon sugar, divided		4	large egg whites, beaten
1	teaspoon ground cinnamon		1	cup skim milk
			1	teaspoon vanilla extract
			1	(16-ounce) loaf French bread, sliced in 1-inch slices

Preheat oven to 350 degrees. In an oblong 2-quart casserole, put berries, ¾ cup sugar, and cinnamon. In a large bowl combine egg, egg whites, milk, and vanilla. Add bread and soak for 5 minutes turning half way through. Arrange bread in one layer over berries. Sprinkle with remaining sugar. Bake for 25 to 30 minutes or until bread is golden. Serve with berry juice and berries.

Makes 8 servings

Doc's Notes:

Breakfast foods can be eaten in the morning or evening. The berries provide a good source of Vitamin C and potassium, and fiber is in relatively good supply, too.

NUTRITIONAL INFORMATION PER SERVING

Calories	304	Saturated Fat (g)	1
Protein (g)	9	Dietary Fiber (g)	4
Carbohydrate (g)	61	Cholesterol (mg)	27
Fat (g)	3	Sodium (mg)	400
Cal. from Fat (%)	8		

Diabetic Exchanges: 0.5 very lean meat, 2 starch, 0.5 fruit, 1.5 other carb.

BAKED FRENCH TOAST

The orange juice and maple syrup
make this a light, not-too-sweet dish.

3 tablespoons margarine, melted	4 large egg whites
⅓ cup maple syrup	1 cup orange juice
1 teaspoon ground cinnamon	8 slices white or whole wheat bread
1 large egg	

Preheat oven to 375 degrees. Combine the margarine and syrup together in a 13x9x2-inch baking pan and sprinkle with the cinnamon. In a mixing bowl, beat together the egg, egg whites, and orange juice. Dip the bread into the egg mixture and arrange in single layer in the baking pan. Bake for 20 to 25 minutes, or until the bread is light brown.

Makes 8 serving

Doc's Notes:
Beware of the orange juice if your mouth is sore.

NUTRITIONAL INFORMATION PER SERVING

Calories	185	Saturated Fat (g)	1
Protein (g)	5	Dietary Fiber (g)	1
Carbohydrate (g)	28	Cholesterol (mg)	27
Fat (g)	6	Sodium (mg)	248
Cal. from Fat (%)	29		

Diabetic Exchanges: 1 starch, 0.5 fruit, 0.5 other carb., 1 fat

APPLE LASAGNA

Apples and pasta pair up for this unusual combo.
Wonderful for breakfast, a light dinner, or even as a side.

8　lasagna noodles
2　(21-ounce) cans apple pie
　　filling
1　(15-ounce) container part
　　skim ricotta cheese
2　large egg whites
1　teaspoon almond extract

¼　cup sugar
⅓　cup all-purpose flour
1　teaspoon ground cinnamon
3　tablespoons margarine
⅓　cup light brown sugar
⅓　cup old-fashioned oatmeal
½　teaspoon vanilla extract

Preheat oven to 350 degrees. Prepare lasagna noodles according to package directions; drain. Spread one can apple pie filling in a 13x9x2-inch pan coated with nonstick cooking spray, slicing any extra-thick apples. Cover apples with four lasagna noodles. In a bowl, mix together ricotta cheese, egg whites, almond extract, and sugar. Spread evenly over lasagna noodles and top with the remaining four lasagna noodles. Spoon remaining can of apple pie filling over lasagna. In a small bowl, crumble together flour, cinnamon, margarine, brown sugar, oatmeal, and vanilla. Sprinkle over apple filling. Bake for 45 minutes. Let stand 15 minutes.

Makes 10 to 12 servings

Doc's Notes:
This can also serve as a dessert or midday snack. The apples are a good source of fiber.

NUTRITIONAL INFORMATION PER SERVING

Calories	292	Saturated Fat (g)	2
Protein (g)	7	Dietary Fiber (g)	2
Carbohydrate (g)	53	Cholesterol (mg)	11
Fat (g)	6	Sodium (mg)	133
Cal. from Fat (%)	19		

Diabetic Exchanges: 0.5 very lean meat, 1 starch, 2 fruit, 0.5 other carb., 1 fat

BREAD PUDDING FLORENTINE

Adjust the mushrooms and onions to your taste buds. Here's a great make-ahead dish. Pop in a cold oven if using a glass dish when baking. Breakfast type foods are enjoyed all times of day.

5 large eggs	1 teaspoon minced garlic
4 large egg whites	1 onion, chopped
3 cups skim milk	2 (10-ounce) boxes frozen
¼ cup Dijon mustard	chopped spinach, thawed
Salt and pepper to taste	and squeezed dry
1 (16-ounce) loaf day-old	1 tablespoon all-purpose
French bread, cut into 16	flour
slices, divided	Salt and pepper to taste
½ pound mushrooms, sliced	1½ cups shredded reduced-fat
	Swiss cheese, divided

In a mixing bowl beat eggs and egg whites with milk, mustard, salt, and pepper; set aside. Place half the bread slices in a 13x9x2-inch baking dish coated with nonstick cooking spray. In a skillet coated with nonstick cooking spray, sauté the mushrooms, garlic, and onion until tender. Add the spinach and flour, stirring to mix well. Season with salt and pepper to taste. Spread mixture over bread. Sprinkle with 1 cup cheese. Top with remaining bread. Sprinkle with remaining ½ cup cheese. Pour egg mixture over casserole and refrigerate 2 hours or overnight. Bake at 350 degrees for 40 to 50 minutes or until puffed and golden.

Makes 10 to 12 servings

Doc's Notes:

This is a great dish to try several days before your next cycle of treatment. Good source of vitamins and minerals.

NUTRITIONAL INFORMATION PER SERVING

Calories	240	Saturated Fat (g)	3
Protein (g)	16	Dietary Fiber (g)	3
Carbohydrate (g)	28	Cholesterol (mg)	101
Fat (g)	7	Sodium (mg)	482
Cal. from Fat (%)	26		

Diabetic Exchanges: 1 very lean meat, 1.5 starch, 1 vegetable, 1 fat

EGG SOUFFLÉ

Leave out the pepper and onions for a plain version of a cheesy egg dish.

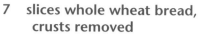
7 slices whole wheat bread, crusts removed
1 red bell pepper, cored and chopped
1 bunch green onions (scallions), chopped
6 ounces reduced fat sharp Cheddar cheese, shredded
6 ounces reduced fat Monterey Jack cheese, shredded

5 large eggs
4 large egg whites
3 cups skim milk
2 tablespoons margarine, melted
1 teaspoon dry mustard
1 teaspoon Worcestershire sauce, optional
Salt and pepper to taste

Line bottom of a 3-quart or 13x9x2-inch baking dish with slices of bread. Cover with chopped red peppers and green onions. Sprinkle with shredded cheeses. In bowl, mix remaining ingredients and pour mixture over cheeses. Refrigerate for 6 hours or overnight. Preheat oven to 350 degrees. Bake for 45 minutes to 1 hour.

Makes 12 servings

Doc's Notes:

This is a great breakfast dish. You might cut this recipe in half. Breakfast foods seem to be the best tolerated of all foods while you are having chemotherapy.

NUTRITIONAL INFORMATION PER SERVING

Calories	197	Saturated Fat (g)	4
Protein (g)	16	Dietary Fiber (g)	1
Carbohydrate (g)	11	Cholesterol (mg)	105
Fat (g)	10	Sodium (mg)	358
Cal. from Fat (%)	45		

Diabetic Exchanges: 2 lean meat, 0.5 starch, 1 fat

EGG NOODLE CASSEROLE

The simple combination of noodles, eggs, and a white sauce translate into a great breakfast dish that can be made ahead.

1   (8-ounce) package wide
    noodles
¼   cup all-purpose flour
2   cups skim milk
1   teaspoon Worcestershire
    sauce

Salt and pepper to taste
½   teaspoon garlic powder
6   hard-boiled large eggs,
    whites only, chopped
⅔   cup shredded reduced-fat
    Cheddar cheese

Preheat oven to 350 degrees. Cook the noodles according to package directions, omitting any salt and oil. Drain; set aside. In a small saucepan, mix together the flour and milk. Cook over a medium heat, stirring, until thickened. Add the Worcestershire sauce, salt and pepper, and garlic powder. Arrange half of the egg whites in the bottom of a 2-quart casserole dish coated with nonstick cooking spray. Cover the egg whites with half of the noodles, then add half the cheese, then half the white sauce. Repeat layers. Bake for 30 minutes.

Makes 6 servings

Doc's Notes:
Use this dish for breakfast, lunch, or dinner. Remember, if it appeals to you at the time, it is OK to eat it whenever. The eggs provide a great source of protein, vitamins, and minerals while the cheese adds protein and calcium.

NUTRITIONAL INFORMATION PER SERVING

Calories 245
Protein (g) 16
Carbohydrate (g) 36
Fat (g) 4
Cal. from Fat (%)................... 15
Saturated Fat (g) 2
Dietary Fiber (g) 1
Cholesterol (mg) 44
Sodium (mg) 194

Diabetic Exchanges: 1 lean meat, 2 starch, 0.5 skim milk

CRABMEAT EGG CASSEROLE

Crabmeat lovers will enjoy this delicious brunch dish.
White or claw crabmeat can be used.
Adjust the chopped veggies to what you can tolerate.

6   slices whole wheat bread
½   cup water
1   tablespoon margarine,
     melted
1   onion, chopped
½   cup chopped green bell
     pepper
½   cup chopped celery
2   cloves garlic, minced

8   ounces reduced fat sharp
     Cheddar cheese, shredded
1   pound lump crabmeat,
     picked for bones
1   large egg
2   large egg whites
½   cup nonfat plain yogurt
Salt and pepper to taste

Preheat oven to 350 degrees. Place bread in a bowl with ½ cup water. Let stand 15 minutes. In a skillet coated with nonstick cooking spray, melt margarine and sauté onion, green pepper, celery, and garlic until tender. Add shredded cheese to bread and water mixture, stirring together. Carefully stir in sautéed vegetables, and crabmeat. In a mixing bowl, beat egg, egg whites, yogurt, and salt and pepper. Combine with crabmeat mixture, mixing well. Transfer into a 2-quart baking dish and bake for 30 to 40 minutes.

Makes 10 servings

Doc's Notes:

This is a meal in one. Add a fruit salad and you are set for the day!

NUTRITIONAL INFORMATION PER SERVING

Calories 205
Protein (g) 21
Carbohydrate (g) 14
Fat (g) 7
Cal. from Fat (%) 31
Saturated Fat (g) 3
Dietary Fiber (g) 3
Cholesterol (mg) 68
Sodium (mg) 454

Diabetic Exchanges: 2.5 lean meat, 0.5 starch, 1 vegetable

STRAWBERRY SOUP

Strawberries offer a high antioxidant profile and vitamin C.

1 quart strawberries, hulled
Juice of 1 orange
3 tablespoons confectioners' sugar

1 (12-ounce) can peach nectar
1½ cups nonfat plain yogurt

In a food processor, combine strawberries and orange juice; blend until smooth. Add the sugar. Gradually add the peach nectar, blending well. Add yogurt, blending until mixed. Refrigerate.

Makes five (1-cup) servings

Doc's Notes:
A light lunch; goes well 2 to 3 days post chemotherapy.

NUTRITIONAL INFORMATION PER SERVING

Calories 139	Saturated Fat (g) 0
Protein (g) 5	Dietary Fiber (g) 3
Carbohydrate (g) 30	Cholesterol (mg) 1
Fat (g) 1	Sodium (mg) 63
Cal. from Fat (%) 4	

Diabetic Exchanges: 1.5 fruit, 0.5 skim milk

PEACH SOUP

Canned peaches may be used.

1½ pounds peaches, peeled,
**   pitted and sliced**
2   cups nonfat plain yogurt
1   cup orange juice

1   cup pineapple juice
1   tablespoon lemon juice
2   tablespoons sugar
¼   cup sherry, optional

Purée peaches in a food processor until smooth. Add all remaining ingredients and blend well. Refrigerate to serve chilled.

Makes 10 servings

Doc's Notes:
Source of Vitamin C, calcium, protein, riboflavin, phosphorus, and B12.

NUTRITIONAL INFORMATION PER SERVING

Calories 89	Saturated Fat (g) 0
Protein (g) 3	Dietary Fiber (g) 1
Carbohydrate (g) 18	Cholesterol (mg) 0
Fat (g) 0	Sodium (mg) 39
Cal. from Fat (%) 0	

Diabetic Exchanges: 1 fruit, 0.5 skim milk

ASPARAGUS AND POTATO SOUP

*By combining the ever popular potato soup with asparagus,
you have a glorious creation. Serve hot or cold.*

4 cups diced peeled red
  potatoes (about 3)
1 cup chopped onion
4 (14½-ounce) cans cut
  asparagus, drained,
  reserving liquid

1 teaspoon minced garlic
1 (12-ounce) can evaporated
  skimmed milk
Salt and pepper to taste

In a large pot, combine potatoes and onion in salted water and bring
to a boil. Reduce heat and cook about 15 minutes or until tender,
drain. Drain cans of asparagus, reserving the juice from two of the
cans. Combine potatoes, onion, asparagus, and garlic in large bowl.
Using a food processor, process the asparagus/potato mixture in batches
until entire mixture is puréed. Add the milk, reserved asparagus juice if
needed to thin, and salt and pepper. Refrigerate.

Makes eight (1-cup) servings

Doc's Notes:
Rich in Vitamin C.

NUTRITIONAL INFORMATION PER SERVING

Calories 136
Protein (g) 9
Carbohydrate (g) 26
Fat (g) 1
Cal. from Fat (%) 4

Saturated Fat (g) 0
Dietary Fiber (g) 4
Cholesterol (mg) 2
Sodium (mg) 644

Diabetic Exchanges: 1 starch, 0.5 skim milk, 1 vegetable

CHICKEN SOUP

Chicken soup is healing and also freezes well. To reduce the sodium, leave out some or all of the bouillon cubes.

4 quarts water
3 pounds skinless, boneless chicken breasts, cut into pieces
1 large onion, cut into wedges
6 sprigs of parsley
3 bay leaves
2 cloves garlic, halved
1 (16-ounce) package baby carrots
1 cup chopped celery
1 turnip, cut into chunks
Salt and pepper to taste
4 chicken bouillon cubes
Cooked rice or noodles, optional

Place all ingredients except rice or noodles in a large pot. Bring to a boil. Reduce the heat, cover, and simmer 45 minutes, or until the chicken is tender. If desired, remove the chicken, carrots, celery, and turnip from the broth and strain the soup. Add the rice or noodles, if desired, and heat through.

Makes eight to ten (1-cup) servings

Doc's Notes:
This makes a great meal 3 to 4 days following chemotherapy.

NUTRITIONAL INFORMATION PER SERVING

Calories	188	Saturated Fat (g)	1
Protein (g)	33	Dietary Fiber (g)	2
Carbohydrate (g)	8	Cholesterol (mg)	79
Fat (g)	2	Sodium (mg)	570
Cal. from Fat (%)	12		

Diabetic Exchanges: 4 very lean meat, 1.5 vegetable

CHICKEN, BARLEY, AND BOW-TIE SOUP

This hearty version of a favorite remedy with barley
and pasta quickly became a favorite in my house.

2½ pounds skinless, boneless chicken breasts, cut into 1-inch pieces
1 cup chopped celery
1½ cups chopped onion
2 cups thinly sliced carrots
1 bay leaf

12 cups water
½ cup pearl barley
Salt and pepper to taste
½ teaspoon dried basil leaves
3 chicken bouillon cubes
1 (16-ounce) package bow-tie pasta

Place the chicken, celery, onion, carrots, bay leaf, and 12 cups water in a large pot. Bring to a boil and add the barley. Reduce the heat, cover, and cook until the chicken and barley are done, about 30 minutes. Season with salt and pepper, and add the basil and bouillon cubes. Meanwhile, cook the pasta according to package directions, omitting oil and salt. Drain and set aside. Remove the bay leaf and add the pasta.

Makes 10 to 12 servings

Doc's Notes:

This goes great any time post-treatment. Barley is a whole grain and a high fiber substitute for rice or pasta.

NUTRITIONAL INFORMATION PER SERVING

Calories 296
Protein (g) 28
Carbohydrate (g) 39
Fat (g) 2
Cal. from Fat (%) 7
Saturated Fat (g) 1
Dietary Fiber (g) 3
Cholesterol (mg) 55
Sodium (mg) 360

Diabetic Exchanges: 2.5 very lean meat, 2.5 starch, 1 vegetable

FRUITY COUSCOUS SALAD

Couscous is made from semolina and is found in your local grocery store. Couscous is easily prepared to create this wonderful salad.

2 cups canned fat-free chicken broth
2 cups couscous
½ cup dried tart cherries or dried cranberries
⅔ cup coarsely chopped carrots
1 cup chopped unpeeled cucumber
1 bunch green onions (scallions), sliced
¼ cup pine nuts or slivered almonds, toasted, optional
3 tablespoons balsamic vinegar
1 tablespoon olive oil
1 tablespoon Dijon mustard
Salt and pepper to taste

Bring broth to a boil in a medium saucepan; stir in couscous. Remove from heat; let stand, covered, 5 minutes. Fluff with a fork. Uncover; cool 10 minutes. Combine cooked couscous, dried fruit, carrots, cucumber, green onions, and pine nuts in a large bowl; mix well. Combine vinegar, olive oil, and mustard in a small bowl; mix well. Pour dressing mixture over couscous mixture; stir to coat all ingredients. Season with salt and pepper, if desired. Serve chilled or at room temperature.

Makes 8 cups, 10 to 12 servings

Doc's Notes:

Carrots provide potassium and beta carotene. Carrots may lower blood cholesterol. The dried fruit also adds fiber and potassium.

NUTRITIONAL INFORMATION PER SERVING

Calories	144	Saturated Fat (g)	0
Protein (g)	5	Dietary Fiber (g)	2
Carbohydrate (g)	29	Cholesterol (mg)	0
Fat (g)	1	Sodium (mg)	141
Cal. from Fat (%)	8		

Diabetic Exchanges: 1.5 starch, 0.5 fruit

WALDORF PASTA SALAD

*This light colorful salad is like eating a fruit salad
with pasta. Top with grilled chicken for a hearty salad.*

8 ounces bow tie pasta
1 cup nonfat plain yogurt
¼ cup frozen orange juice
   concentrate
1 (11-ounce) can mandarin
   orange slices, drained

1 cup seedless red grapes,
   halved
1 green apple, cored and
   chopped
1 cup chopped celery

Prepare the pasta according to package directions; set aside. In a small
bowl, blend the yogurt with the orange juice. In a large bowl, combine the pasta, mandarin orange slices, grapes, apple, and celery. Stir
in the yogurt mixture; toss well. Cover and refrigerate until chilled.

Makes 6 servings

Doc's Notes:
This is a full meal in one dish. The fruit are great sources of fiber.
Red grapes are a source of resveratrol which is a phytochemical or
cancer protective substance.

NUTRITIONAL INFORMATION PER SERVING

Calories	235	Saturated Fat (g)	0
Protein (g)	8	Dietary Fiber (g)	3
Carbohydrate (g)	50	Cholesterol (mg)	1
Fat (g)	1	Sodium (mg)	53
Cal. from Fat (%)	3		

Diabetic Exchanges: 2 starch, 1 fruit, 0.5 skim milk

TUNA SALAD

Canned tuna turned into a delightful dish.

2   (6-ounce) cans white tuna, packed in water, drained
1   (11-ounce) can mandarin oranges, drained
¼   pound fresh mushrooms, sliced
1   (14-ounce) can artichoke hearts, drained and cut in half
1   (8-ounce) can sliced water chestnuts, drained

Carefully combine all ingredients in large bowl. Toss with Dressing (recipe follows). Serve immediately.

Dressing

¼   cup fat-free or low fat mayonnaise
¼   cup nonfat plain yogurt
1   tablespoon lemon juice
2   teaspoons sugar
1   bunch green onions (scallions), thinly sliced

Combine all ingredients together and fold into tuna mixture.

Makes 8 servings

Doc's Notes:

Great salad on those hot summer days. Good source of fiber, Vitamin C, B, copper, and other minerals.

NUTRITIONAL INFORMATION PER SERVING

Calories 111
Protein (g) 12
Carbohydrate (g) 12
Fat (g) 2
Cal. from Fat (%) 13
Saturated Fat (g) 0
Dietary Fiber (g) 2
Cholesterol (mg) 19
Sodium (mg) 323

Diabetic Exchanges: 1.5 very lean meat, 2 vegetable

PERFECT PASTA

Takes angel hair to a new level.

1   (12-ounce) package angel   2   cloves garlic, minced
    hair pasta   1   tablespoon finely chopped
3   tablespoons olive oil   parsley

Cook pasta according to directions on package, omitting salt and oil. Drain and set aside. In a small pan, combine all remaining ingredients and sauté for a few minutes. Pour over cooked pasta and toss. Serve immediately.

Makes 6 to 8 servings

Doc's Notes:
Good anytime post-treatment.

NUTRITIONAL INFORMATION PER SERVING

Calories	204	Saturated Fat (g)	1
Protein (g)	6	Dietary Fiber (g)	1
Carbohydrate (g)	32	Cholesterol (mg)	0
Fat (g)	6	Sodium (mg)	3
Cal. from Fat (%)	26		

Diabetic Exchanges: 1 starch, 1 fat

POTATO PIZZA

Instead of mashed or baked potatoes, try this version.
Adjust the recipe for your family by adding different cheeses
or leaving off the onions…serve with a dollop of plain yogurt.

4   baking potatoes, peeled and cut into ¼-inch thick round slices
1   tablespoon minced garlic
2   tablespoons olive oil

Salt and pepper to taste
½   cup chopped green onions (scallions)
½   cup shredded reduced-fat Cheddar cheese

Preheat oven to 350 degrees. In a large bowl, mix together the potato slices, garlic, olive oil, and salt and pepper. Coat a 12-inch pizza pan with nonstick cooking spray and arrange the potato slices to cover the pizza pan, overlapping the slices. Bake for 35 to 40 minutes or until the potato slices are tender. Remove from the oven and sprinkle with the green onions and cheese. Return to the oven and continue baking 5 minutes longer or until the cheese is melted.

Makes 6 to 8 servings

NUTRITIONAL INFORMATION PER SERVING

Calories	104	Saturated Fat (g)	1
Protein (g)	4	Dietary Fiber (g)	2
Carbohydrate (g)	14	Cholesterol (mg)	4
Fat (g)	5	Sodium (mg)	46
Cal. from Fat (%)	37		

Diabetic Exchanges: 1 starch, 1 fat

CHEESY MACARONI

A comfort food that we are never too old to enjoy.
The cheeses are high in calcium and protein.
Add more milk if needed to thin.

1   (16-ounce) package elbow
   macaroni
2   tablespoons cornstarch
2   cups skim milk

1   (8-ounce) package reduced-
   fat sharp Cheddar cheese,
   cut into chunks
1   (16-ounce) container
   reduced fat cottage cheese
Salt and pepper to taste

Cook pasta according to package directions, drain. In a large pot, mix together cornstarch and milk over medium heat, stirring until thickened. Add Cheddar cheese, stirring until melted. Add pasta, tossing until well combined and heated. In a food processor, blend cottage cheese until smooth. Add to pasta mixture. Season with salt and pepper.

Makes 8 servings

Doc's Notes:
A higher calorie and good source of protein and calcium recipe. This makes a great light main dish.

NUTRITIONAL INFORMATION PER SERVING

Calories	360	Saturated Fat (g)	4
Protein (g)	24	Dietary Fiber (g)	1
Carbohydrate (g)	49	Cholesterol (mg)	24
Fat (g)	7	Sodium (mg)	405
Cal. from Fat (%)	17		

Diabetic Exchanges: 2 lean meat, 3 starch, 0.5 skim milk

ORZO ASPARAGUS TOSS

*Asparagus adds spunk to this Italian pasta dish. Orzo is
a rice shaped pasta. Substitute any pasta for this dish.*

1 (16-ounce) package orzo	1 cup thinly sliced onion
2 tablespoons olive oil	1 tablespoon finely minced
2 cups asparagus spears, cut	garlic
in 2-inch pieces	1 cup tomato chunks
1 red bell pepper, cored and	⅓ cup grated Romano cheese,
cut in strips	optional

Cook orzo according to directions on package. Drain and set aside.
Meanwhile, in a large skillet, heat olive oil and sauté the asparagus,
red pepper, onion, garlic, and tomato until all are tender. Add cooked
orzo and toss together. If desired, add the Romano cheese.

Makes 6 servings

Doc's Notes:

This is another healthful, easy to fix meal and adjust pepper, onion, and tomato to how you feel. Serve with grilled chicken breast
and whole wheat toast for a complete meal.

NUTRITIONAL INFORMATION PER SERVING

Calories	354	Saturated Fat (g)	1
Protein (g)	12	Dietary Fiber (g)	4
Carbohydrate (g)	64	Cholesterol (mg)	0
Fat (g)	6	Sodium (mg)	10
Cal. from Fat (%)	15		

Diabetic Exchanges: 4 starch, 1 vegetable, 0.5 fat

SIMPLY DELICIOUS CHICKEN

When I was testing recipes my family made me promise to repeat this dish often. The simplicity of the dish is very appealing.

2   pounds boneless skinless chicken breasts
⅓   cup all-purpose flour
Salt and pepper to taste
2   tablespoons olive oil

1   cup canned fat-free chicken broth
1   tablespoon cornstarch
Juice of ½ lemon
2   tablespoons chopped parsley

Dust the chicken breasts with flour and salt and pepper. In large skillet, sauté the chicken in olive oil until brown and almost done. Mix together the chicken broth and cornstarch; add to the skillet. Stir in the lemon juice. Sprinkle with parsley before serving.

Makes 8 servings

Doc's Notes:
Nutritious yet simple and elegant and low fat. Anyone in the house can prepare this main course.

NUTRITIONAL INFORMATION PER SERVING

Calories 180
Protein (g) 27
Carbohydrate (g) 5
Fat (g) 5
Cal. from Fat (%) 25

Saturated Fat (g) 1
Dietary Fiber (g) 0
Cholesterol (mg) 66
Sodium (mg) 152

Diabetic Exchanges: 3 very lean meat, 0.5 starch

CHICKEN DIANE WITH WILD RICE

This light chicken entrée has the taste and flair of a gourmet dish without all the complication. Mushrooms are nutritious; they contain some protein, vitamins, and minerals. Try using the different varieties.

¾ pound mushrooms, sliced
1 cup chopped onion
1½ pounds skinless, boneless chicken breasts
Salt and pepper to taste
¼ cup chopped green onion (scallion) stems (green part only)
2 tablespoons chopped parsley

1 cup canned fat-free chicken broth
3 tablespoons sherry, optional
1½ tablespoons Dijon mustard
1 (6-ounce) box long-grain and wild rice
1 (14-ounce) can artichoke heart quarters, drained

Coat a large skillet with nonstick cooking spray and sauté the mushrooms and onion over medium heat until tender, about 5 minutes. Remove from the skillet; set aside. Sprinkle the chicken breasts with salt and pepper. In the same skillet coated with nonstick cooking spray, cook the chicken until lightly browned on both sides, about 5 to 7 minutes. Spoon the reserved mushroom mixture over the chicken in the pan. Combine the green onions, parsley, chicken broth, sherry, and Dijon mustard in a small bowl and pour over the chicken. Cover, reduce the heat, and simmer 20 minutes or until the chicken is tender. Meanwhile, prepare the rice according to the package directions. Toss the cooked rice with the artichoke hearts. Serve the chicken and sauce on top of the rice.

Makes 4 to 6 servings

Doc's Notes:
A little sherry will not hurt you. Enjoy!

NUTRITIONAL INFORMATION PER SERVING

Calories	274	Saturated Fat (g)	0
Protein (g)	32	Dietary Fiber (g)	2
Carbohydrate (g)	30	Cholesterol (mg)	66
Fat (g)	2	Sodium (mg)	810
Cal. from Fat (%)	6		

Diabetic Exchanges: 3 very lean meat, 1.5 starch, 1.5 vegetable

ITALIAN CHICKEN

This is way too easy to be so good! The
Italian herbs give that finishing touch.

1 (6-ounce) box long grain
and wild rice mix
¾ cup water
1 (14½-ounce) can diced
tomatoes
½ cup shredded part-skim
mozzarella cheese
2 teaspoons dried basil
leaves, divided

2 teaspoons dried oregano
leaves, divided
1 teaspoon minced garlic
1½ pounds skinless, boneless
chicken breasts, cut into
strips
¼ cup grated Parmesan
cheese

Preheat oven to 375 degrees. In a 2- to 3-quart oblong baking dish coated with nonstick cooking spray, combine the water, rice, seasoning packet, tomatoes, mozzarella, 1 teaspoon basil, 1 teaspoon oregano, and garlic, stirring well. Top the rice mixture with the chicken strips and sprinkle with the remaining basil and oregano and the cheese. Bake, covered, for 45 minutes. Uncover and continue baking 15 minutes longer, or until the chicken is tender and the rice is cooked.

Makes 4 servings

Doc's Notes:

This is a great one-dish meal to enjoy during the week prior to your next treatment.

NUTRITIONAL INFORMATION PER SERVING

Calories	430	Saturated Fat (g)	3.2
Protein (g)	50	Dietary Fiber (g)	3
Carbohydrate (g)	40	Cholesterol (mg)	112
Fat (g)	7	Sodium (mg)	1055
Cal. from Fat (%)	14		

Diabetic Exchanges: 5 very lean meat, 2.5 starch, 1 vegetable

QUICK CHICKEN AND DUMPLINGS

The flour tortillas are a great trick to use for no-trouble dumplings and will enhance the chicken soup.

5¼ cups canned fat-free
    chicken broth
5¼ cups water
1½ pounds boneless skinless
    chicken breasts, cut into
    pieces

1 cup sliced carrots
Salt and pepper to taste
10 (6-inch) flour or whole
    wheat tortillas

Pour the chicken broth and water into a large pot. Add the chicken pieces, carrots, and salt and pepper to taste. Bring the mixture to a boil. Reduce the heat to medium and continue to cook for 25 minutes or until the chicken is done and the carrots are tender. Cut the tortillas into small wedges. Add the cut up tortillas to the pot and stir. Continue to cook until the tortillas are tender, about 5 minutes. If you need more liquid in pot, add more broth or water.

Makes 8 to 10 servings

Doc's Notes:
Light and hearty — enjoy at any time during your chemotherapy cycle.

NUTRITIONAL INFORMATION PER SERVING

Calories 178	Saturated Fat (g) 0
Protein (g) 20	Dietary Fiber (g) 0
Carbohydrate (g) 15	Cholesterol (mg) 40
Fat (g) 4	Sodium (mg) 598
Cal. from Fat (%) 20	

Diabetic Exchanges: 2 very lean meat, 1 starch

BAKED FISH

Another quick topping that is outstanding on any fish!

1   pound fish fillets
2   tablespoons light
     mayonnaise or
     mayonnaise of choice
1   teaspoon lemon juice
½   teaspoon prepared mustard
½   teaspoon sugar

¼   teaspoon Worcestershire
     sauce
¼   teaspoon onion powder
¼   teaspoon garlic powder
⅛   teaspoon cayenne pepper,
     optional
Paprika

Rinse fish and pat dry. In a small dish combine remaining ingredients except paprika, mixing well. Lay fish in an oblong baking dish coated with nonstick cooking spray. Spread mayonnaise mixture over fillets. Marinate 30 minutes. Preheat oven to 500 degrees. Sprinkle with paprika. Bake for 10 to 15 minutes or until fish flakes easily with fork.

Makes 4 servings

Doc's Notes:
This is light and easily digested. Great replacement for red meat. Some drugs make you lose your taste for red meat.

NUTRITIONAL INFORMATION PER SERVING

Calories	122	Saturated Fat (g)	1
Protein (g)	20	Dietary Fiber (g)	0
Carbohydrate (g)	2	Cholesterol (mg)	51
Fat (g)	3	Sodium (mg)	133
Cal. from Fat (%)	25		

Diabetic Exchanges: 3 very lean meat

BROILED SHRIMP

When you want a delicious recipe with no clean up, here it is. The pan is lined with foil and no other dishes are used. No effort, yet great taste.

2	pounds peeled large shrimp	½	cup Italian bread crumbs
1	tablespoon minced garlic	¼	cup grated Parmesan
⅓	cup balsamic vinegar		cheese
¼	cup white wine, optional	2	tablespoons olive oil

Preheat the broiler. Lay shrimp on a foil-lined pan. Sprinkle with the garlic, vinegar, and white wine. Sprinkle bread crumbs and Parmesan cheese on top. Drizzle with the olive oil. Let sit for 15 minutes. Place under broiler for about 10 to 15 minutes or until shrimp are done. Watch carefully while cooking.

Makes 8 servings

Doc's Notes:

Great dish to have the week before the next cycle of chemotherapy is scheduled. Serve with a simple green salad, French bread, and a glass of white wine. Shrimp are low in calories and are an excellent source of protein, iron, and trace minerals zinc and copper.

NUTRITIONAL INFORMATION PER SERVING

Calories	203	Saturated Fat (g)	1
Protein (g)	25	Dietary Fiber (g)	0
Carbohydrate (g)	9	Cholesterol (mg)	175
Fat (g)	7	Sodium (mg)	336
Cal. from Fat (%)	31		

Diabetic Exchanges: 3 very lean meat, 0.5 starch, 1 fat

YAM BISCUITS

You can quickly whip up these biscuits with ingredients found in your pantry. By including yams, you're including nutrition. Make larger biscuits to use for sandwiches.

1 (15-ounce) can sweet potatoes (yams), drained and mashed
4 cups all-purpose baking mix
½ teaspoon ground cinnamon
¾ cup skim milk
3 tablespoons margarine, softened

Preheat oven to 450 degrees. In a mixing bowl, mix the mashed yams with the baking mix and cinnamon. Add the milk and margarine to the mixture, stirring until blended. Roll on a floured surface to 1-inch thickness. Cut with a 2-inch cutter or a glass and place on a baking sheet. Bake for 10 to 12 minutes or until golden brown.

Makes 2 dozen

Doc's Notes:
Sweet potatoes are rich in beta carotene, and Vitamins C and B.

NUTRITIONAL INFORMATION PER SERVING

Calories	110	Saturated Fat (g)	1
Protein (g)	2	Dietary Fiber (g)	1
Carbohydrate (g)	16	Cholesterol (mg)	0
Fat (g)	5	Sodium (mg)	282
Cal. from Fat (%)	36		

Diabetic Exchanges: 1 starch, 1 fat

CHESS PIE

Whip up this quick yummy pie when you have a sweet tooth, but want something not too rich. Add lemon extract for a lemon flavor.

2	tablespoons margarine, melted	1	(5-ounce) can evaporated skimmed milk
1	cup sugar	2	large eggs, beaten
3	tablespoons all-purpose flour	1	teaspoon butter extract
		1	(9-inch) pie shell, unbaked

Preheat oven to 350 degrees. Combine the margarine, sugar, flour, evaporated milk, eggs, and butter extract in a bowl, beating well. Pour into the pie shell. Bake for 30 minutes or until firm. Cool before serving.

Makes 6 to 8 servings

Doc's Notes:
A slice or two daily for lunch or dinner will help keep your weight up.

NUTRITIONAL INFORMATION PER SERVING

Calories	249	Saturated Fat (g)	3
Protein (g)	4	Dietary Fiber (g)	0
Carbohydrate (g)	39	Cholesterol (mg)	57
Fat (g)	9	Sodium (mg)	132
Cal. from Fat (%)	31		

Diabetic Exchanges: 1 starch, 1.5 other carb., 1.5 fat

PINEAPPLE BREAD PUDDING
WITH LEMON APRICOT SAUCE

This is best served warm and is quite an indulgent,
yet light dessert. Use the Lemon Apricot Sauce
over fruit or ice cream. Easy on your tummy.

1 (16-ounce) loaf French bread, sliced	1 cup skim milk
1 (20-ounce) can crushed pineapple in juice	¾ cup sugar
	1 teaspoon vanilla extract
	1 teaspoon butter flavoring
2 large eggs	1 teaspoon ground cinnamon
1 large egg white	

Preheat oven to 350 degrees. Lay bread slices in a 2-quart oblong pan coated with nonstick cooking spray. Spread crushed pineapple with juice evenly over bread. In a large bowl, beat together eggs, egg white, milk, sugar, vanilla, butter flavoring, and cinnamon. Pour evenly over pineapple. Bake for 45 minutes.

Lemon Apricot Sauce

⅓ cup sugar	1 (5-ounce) can evaporated fat-free skimmed milk
⅓ cup apricot nectar	
1 teaspoon cornstarch	1 tablespoon lemon juice

Combine sugar and nectar in a small saucepan. Bring to a boil. Combine the cornstarch and evaporated milk in a small bowl. Add to nectar mixture. Return to a boil and cook for 1 minute, stirring constantly. Remove from heat; add lemon juice. Serve over warm bread pudding.

Makes 8 servings

NUTRITIONAL INFORMATION PER SERVING

Calories	359	Saturated Fat (g)	1
Protein (g)	10	Dietary Fiber (g)	3
Carbohydrate (g)	73	Cholesterol (mg)	54
Fat (g)	3	Sodium (mg)	413
Cal. from Fat (%)	8		

Diabetic Exchanges: 0.5 very lean meat, 2 starch, 1 fruit, 2 other carb.

BANANA PUDDING TRIFLE

*Bananas, custard, and vanilla wafers are definitely
comfort foods, yet together form a satisfying special
dessert. For a plainer version, omit the candy.*

⅔ cup sugar
¾ cup all-purpose flour
3½ cups skim milk
2 large egg yolks, slightly
   beaten
1 tablespoon vanilla extract
1 (11-ounce) box reduced-fat
   vanilla wafers, divided

6 bananas, divided
2 (1.4-ounce) English toffee
   candy bars, crushed,
   divided
1 (8-ounce) container fat-free
   frozen whipped topping,
   thawed

In a large saucepan, combine the sugar and flour. Gradually stir in the milk and bring the mixture to a boil over a medium-high heat, stirring constantly. Place the egg yolks in a small bowl and gradually pour some of the hot custard into the egg yolks, mixing well with a fork. Gradually, pour the hot custard mixture back into the saucepan with the remaining custard, cooking over a low heat for several minutes. Do not boil. Remove from the heat and add the vanilla. Transfer the custard to a bowl and allow to cool (can refrigerate to speed up the cooling). In a trifle bowl or large glass bowl, place one-third of the vanilla wafers. Slice 2 of the bananas and place on top the wafers. Spread one-half of the custard on top and sprinkle with one-half of the crushed candy bars. Repeat the layers again using all of the remaining custard and crushed candy bars. Place the final one-third of the vanilla wafers on top. Slice 2 bananas on top of wafers and cover with the whipped topping. Refrigerate at least 1 hour before serving.

Makes 16 servings

Doc's Notes:
This is an excellent source of potassium.

NUTRITIONAL INFORMATION PER SERVING

Calories	255	Saturated Fat (g)	1
Protein (g)	4	Dietary Fiber (g)	1
Carbohydrate (g)	50	Cholesterol (mg)	30
Fat (g)	4	Sodium (mg)	121
Cal. from Fat (%)	14		

Diabetic Exchanges: 1.5 starch, 1 fruit, 1 other carb., 0.5 fat

LEMON ANGEL FOOD CAKE

Serve this cake with assorted fresh berries or a fruit sauce.
As a time saver, you can use a commercially prepared
angel food cake and just omit lemon extract.

1 **(16-ounce) box angel food cake mix**
1 **teaspoon lemon extract**
1 **(6-serving) package vanilla pudding mix**

1 **(8-ounce) container nonfat lemon yogurt**
1 **(8-ounce) container fat free frozen whipped topping, thawed**

Prepare cake according to package directions and adding lemon extract. Bake as directed in an angel food cake pan. Cool upside down over a narrow-neck bottle. In a bowl, blend dry pudding mix with lemon yogurt using a wire whisk. Fold in whipped topping. Remove cake from pan. Slice cake horizontally into 3 layers. Place bottom layer on a serving plate and top with one-third of lemon yogurt mixture. Repeat layers twice. Refrigerate.

Makes 12 servings

Doc's Notes:
Tasty yet very healthful and low in fat.

NUTRITIONAL INFORMATION PER SERVING

Calories	227	Saturated Fat (g)	0
Protein (g)	4	Dietary Fiber (g)	0
Carbohydrate (g)	51	Cholesterol (mg)	0
Fat (g)	0	Sodium (mg)	329
Cal. from Fat (%)	0		

Diabetic Exchanges: 1.5 starch, 2 other carb.

MOCK CHOCOLATE ECLAIR

Requests for graham crackers and
pudding put this recipe high on your list.

2   wrapped packages graham
    crackers (from 16-ounce
    box)
2   (4-serving) packages vanilla
    instant pudding and pie
    filling

3   cups skim milk
½   (8-ounce) container frozen
    fat-free whipped topping

Layer bottom of a 13x9x2-inch baking dish with one-third of graham crackers. In a mixing bowl, beat pudding mix with milk until thickened; let stand for several minutes. Fold in whipped topping. Spread half of pudding mixture over graham crackers. Repeat layers, ending with graham crackers on top (three layers graham crackers). Spread with Chocolate Topping (recipe follows).

Chocolate Topping
¼   cup cocoa
⅔   cup sugar
¼   cup skim milk

1   tablespoon vanilla extract
1   tablespoon margarine

Combine cocoa, sugar, and milk in a saucepan. Bring to a boil for 1 minute. Remove from heat and add vanilla and margarine. Cool slightly and pour over graham crackers. Refrigerate until ready to serve (can be made night before).

Makes 15 to 20 servings

Doc's Notes:
Eat this seven days a week. Easy on the tummy anytime.

NUTRITIONAL INFORMATION PER SERVING

Calories 154	Cal. from Fat (%) 14
Protein (g) 3	Saturated Fat (g) 1
Carbohydrate (g) 31	Dietary Fiber (g) 1
Fat (g) 2	Cholesterol (mg) 1
	Sodium (mg) 253

Diabetic Exchanges: 1 starch, 1 other carb.

NEUTROPENIA
(LOW WHITE BLOOD CELL COUNT)

✤ *What is neutropenia?*

✤ *Do I have to go into isolation?*

✤ *How long does neutropenia last?*

✤ *Is it okay to eat raw fruits and vegetables once neutropenia has subsided?*

Neutropenia, or low white blood cell count, is a common complication following a large number of treatments. Most chemotherapeutic drugs will lower your blood counts to some degree. This is because chemotherapy will destroy good cells such as white blood cells, red blood cells and platelets that are produced in the bone marrow. Our goal with chemotherapy is to destroy cancer cells and allow good cells to regenerate and flourish. Unfortunately, we destroy both good and bad cells after each treatment of chemotherapy. The nausea and vomiting is partially secondary to the destruction of cells lining the gastrointestinal tract. Hair loss is secondary to the destruction of hair follicles.

Neutropenia usually lasts four to seven days. This can vary from person to person and treatment to treatment. Normally, we recommend avoiding crowds and anyone that is ill until your blood counts are normal. Raw fruits, vegetables, meat, and seafood are harbingers of bacteria which, if ingested during the times your white blood cells are low, can lead to a systemic infection and should also be avoided. You can become neutropenic following successive treatments. The neutropenia will only last four to seven days in most cases; however, it can be longer with certain leukemia treatments. Once your counts have recovered you can resume your normal activities and diet.

Again during the period of neutropenia, avoid raw fruits, raw vegetables, raw meat and raw seafood. I hope the recipes that follow will give you directions on what to eat during the time your white blood cell count is down and you are more susceptible to infections.

Points to Remember

- ❖ NO RAW FOOD
- ❖ Cooked fruit or veggies
- ❖ No fresh, frozen, or dried fruit
- ❖ No honey – use molasses
- ❖ Avoid uncooked herbs and spices
- ❖ Processed cheese is acceptable
- ❖ Canned or cooked fruits are acceptable
- ❖ All cooked or baked goods: jello, syrup, ice cream and sherbet made from pasteurized products are acceptable.
- ❖ Yogurt
- ❖ Cooked hot soups
- ❖ All breads, rolls, crackers in wrappers.

MENUS
Foods to eat when neutropenia is occurring

Breakfast
Oatmeal Pancakes (p. 200)

Cinnamon Rolls (p. 23)

Apple Lasagna (p. 27)
Quick Cheese Grits (p. 58)

Baked French Toast (p. 26)

Lunch
Pumpkin Soup (p. 59) or Two-Potato Bisque (p. 61)
Spinach Bread (p. 157)

Chicken Pot Pie (p. 67)
Hot Fruit Compote (p. 70)

Dinner
Chicken Piccata (p. 68)
Linguine Florentine (p. 64)
Mocha Cappuccino Pudding Pie (p. 72)

Baked Topped Fish (p. 226)
Cheesy Macaroni (p. 41)
Chess Pie (p. 50)

Very Good Veal (p. 69)
Carrot Soufflé (p. 143)

Egg Noodle Casserole (p. 30)
Baked Peach Delight (p. 73)

Snacks
Cheese Quesadillas (p. 166)

Artichoke Squares (p. 160)

Hot Cocoa Drink Supplement (p. 76)
or Awesome Milkshake (p. 150)

Mini Cheese Pizzas (p. 162)

QUICK CHEESE GRITS

Sometimes grits just hit the spot. If not serving immediately, reheat, and add milk to make creamy if needed.

4   cups water
1   cup skim milk
½   teaspoon salt
1½ cups quick grits
3   tablespoons margarine

3   cups shredded reduced-fat
      Cheddar cheese
1   tablespoon Worcestershire
      sauce
¼   teaspoon garlic powder

In a saucepan, bring the water, milk, and salt to a boil. Add grits, reduce heat, and cook about 5 minutes, stirring occasionally. Add margarine, cheese, Worcestershire sauce, and garlic powder. Stir until margarine and cheese melts.

Makes 12 servings

Doc's Notes:
For weight gain, don't used reduced-fat products.

NUTRITIONAL INFORMATION PER SERVING

Calories 186
Protein (g) 11
Carbohydrate (g) 17
Fat (g) 8
Cal. from Fat (%) 40

Saturated Fat (g) 4
Dietary Fiber (g) 0
Cholesterol (mg) 15
Sodium (mg) 335

Diabetic Exchanges: 1 lean meat, 1 starch, 1 fat

PUMPKIN SOUP

Here's a quick soup that is especially perfect to serve in the fall.

½ cup finely chopped onion
½ teaspoon minced garlic
1 (15-ounce) can solid pack
    pumpkin

3½ cups canned fat-free
    chicken broth
½ cup skim milk
Salt and pepper to taste
Nonfat plain yogurt

In a pot coated with nonstick cooking spray, sauté the onion and garlic over a medium heat until tender, about 5 minutes. Add the pumpkin. Gradually add the chicken broth and milk. Season with salt and pepper. Cook until heated through, about 5 minutes. Serve with a dollop of yogurt.

Makes six (1-cup) servings

Doc's Notes:
Onions provide Vitamin C and folacin while the pumpkin provides beta carotene and Vitamin C.

NUTRITIONAL INFORMATION PER SERVING

Calories	45	Saturated Fat (g)	0
Protein (g)	4	Dietary Fiber (g)	3
Carbohydrate (g)	8	Cholesterol (mg)	0
Fat (g)	0	Sodium (mg)	391
Cal. from Fat (%)	0		

Diabetic Exchanges: 0.5 starch

CHEESE BROCCOLI SOUP

Broccoli is disguised in this nutritious creamy cheesy soup.

2 tablespoons margarine
1 onion, chopped
½ cup all-purpose flour
3 cups canned fat-free
   chicken broth
2 (10-ounce) packages frozen
   chopped broccoli, thawed
   and drained

1½ cups skim milk
4 ounces light pasteurized
   processed cheese spread,
   cut into cubes
Salt and pepper to taste

In a large saucepan, melt the margarine and sauté the onion until tender, about 5 minutes. Blend in the flour, stirring. Gradually add the chicken broth and then the broccoli, stirring to combine. Bring the mixture to a boil, stirring. Reduce heat to low. Cover and cook for 15 to 20 minutes or until the broccoli is done and the soup thickens. Add the milk, stirring until blended. Add the cheese cubes to the soup, stirring and cooking over a low heat until the cheese is melted and smooth. Season to taste. If you want a cheesier soup, just add extra cheese.

Makes 6 to 8 servings

Doc's Notes:

This soup is hearty and healthy. Broccoli is not only a good source of Vitamin C and beta carotene, it also contains nitrogen compounds called indoles, which may be protective against certain forms of cancer. As long as the veggies are cooked, enjoy!

NUTRITIONAL INFORMATION PER SERVING

Calories	135	Saturated Fat (g)	2
Protein (g)	9	Dietary Fiber (g)	3
Carbohydrate (g)	16	Cholesterol (mg)	7
Fat (g)	5	Sodium (mg)	527
Cal. from Fat (%)	30		

Diabetic Exchanges: 0.5 lean meat, 0.5 starch, 1 vegetable, 1 fat

TWO-POTATO BISQUE

Here's a different and delicious twist on bisque.

1 large sweet potato (yam), peeled and cut into 1-inch cubes
1 large baking potato, peeled and cut into 1-inch cubes
1 onion, chopped
2 cloves garlic, minced
1 bay leaf

Salt to taste
1 teaspoon dried thyme leaves
2 cups canned fat-free chicken broth
1 cup buttermilk
1 cup skim milk
2 tablespoons lime juice

In a large pot, combine the sweet potato, baking potato, onion, garlic, bay leaf, salt, thyme, and chicken broth and bring to a boil. Reduce the heat and simmer, covered, for 15 minutes, or until the potatoes are tender. Pour the mixture into a food processor and blend until smooth; return to the pot. Add the buttermilk, skim milk, and lime juice and cook over a low heat just until heated through; do not boil. Remove bay leaf before serving.

Makes 4 to 6 serving

NUTRITIONAL INFORMATION PER SERVING

Calories 100
Protein (g) 6
Carbohydrate (g) 20
Fat (g) 0
Cal. from Fat (%) 0

Saturated Fat (g) 0
Dietary Fiber (g) 2
Cholesterol (mg) 0
Sodium (mg) 281

Diabetic Exchanges: 1 starch, 0.5 skim milk

ARTICHOKE SOUP

A few cans thrown in the food processor
makes a wonderful creamy creation.

3 (14-ounce) cans artichoke hearts, drained
3 (10¾-ounce) cans fat-free cream of mushroom soup
1 cup skim milk

2 cups canned fat-free chicken broth
½ cup dry white wine, optional

Place artichokes in a food processor and purée. Combine remaining ingredients in a bowl and add to processor. Blend until well combined. Transfer to a pot and heat over low heat to serve.

Makes 6 to 8 servings

Doc's Notes:
This can be served at room temperature. Artichokes are high in Vitamin C, folacin, magnesium, phosphorus, and potassium. Artichokes offer a health protective substance called silymarin, which may play a role in cancer prevention.

NUTRITIONAL INFORMATION PER SERVING

Calories 112
Protein (g) 5
Carbohydrate (g) 17
Fat (g) 3
Cal. from Fat (%).................. 23

Saturated Fat (g) 1
Dietary Fiber (g) 1
Cholesterol (mg) 5
Sodium (mg).................... 1200

Diabetic Exchanges: 0.5 starch, 0.5 vegetable, 0.5 fat

EASY CRAB SOUP

A quick version when in a pinch!

1   onion, finely chopped
2   tablespoons margarine
2   tablespoons all-purpose
    flour
1¾ cups canned fat-free
    chicken broth
½   cup water

1   (12-ounce) can evaporated
    skimmed milk
1   pound lump or white
    crabmeat, picked for bones
3   green onion stems
    (scallions), finely sliced,
    optional

In a saucepan, sauté onion in margarine until tender. Stir in flour and gradually add broth and water. Simmer for 20 minutes on low heat. Stir in milk. Fold in crabmeat. Garnish with green onion stems when not neutropenic.

Makes 4 servings

Doc's Notes:
Use green onion as a garnish only when not neutropenic.

NUTRITIONAL INFORMATION PER SERVING

Calories	286	Saturated Fat (g)	1
Protein (g)	35	Dietary Fiber (g)	1
Carbohydrate (g)	19	Cholesterol (mg)	90
Fat (g)	7	Sodium (mg)	888
Cal. from Fat (%)	23		

Diabetic Exchanges: 4 very lean meat, 1 skim milk, 1 vegetable, 1 fat

LINGUINE FLORENTINE

This simply seasoned dish proved to be a light but satisfying dinner.

2	tablespoons olive oil		Salt and pepper to taste
1	teaspoon minced garlic	1	(16-ounce) package
1	large bunch fresh spinach, (5 to 6 cups), stemmed and washed		linguine
		⅓	cup grated Parmesan cheese
1	(12-ounce) can evaporated skimmed milk		

In a large skillet, heat the oil and add the garlic and spinach. Cover and cook until the spinach is wilted, about 3 minutes, stirring occasionally. Add the milk and season to taste. Meanwhile, prepare the pasta according to package directions; drain. Toss with the spinach in the skillet and sprinkle with the cheese.

Makes 6 servings

Doc's Notes:

Add baked or grilled fish on the side and you have a wonderful meal! Cooked veggies are fine when white blood cell count is low.

NUTRITIONAL INFORMATION PER SERVING

Calories	402	Saturated Fat (g)	2
Protein (g)	18	Dietary Fiber (g)	3
Carbohydrate (g)	65	Cholesterol (mg)	7
Fat (g)	8	Sodium (mg)	202
Cal. from Fat (%)	17		

Diabetic Exchanges: 4 starch, 0.5 skim milk, 1 fat

LOADED POTATOES

These yummy potatoes can be served plain or add your favorite condiments depending on your taste tolerance.

1 (32-ounce) bag frozen hash brown potatoes
2 large eggs
3 large egg whites
2 cups skim milk
4 tablespoons margarine, melted
Salt and pepper to taste

½ teaspoon onion powder
2 cups shredded reduced-fat Cheddar cheese
½ cup nonfat plain yogurt
½ cup sliced green onions (scallions), optional
½ cup salsa, optional

Preheat oven to 350 degrees. Place the potatoes in a 1½-quart shallow baking dish coated with nonstick cooking spray. Bake for 15 minutes. Meanwhile, combine the eggs, egg whites, milk, margarine, salt and pepper, and onion powder. Remove the potatoes from the oven. Sprinkle with the Cheddar cheese, tossing toss with a fork to mix. Pour the milk mixture over the potatoes. Return to the oven and bake for 30 to 40 minutes longer or until the potatoes are light brown and firm to touch. Serve with green onions and salsa.

Makes 6 servings

Doc's Notes:
If neutropenic, don't use salsa or green onions.

NUTRITIONAL INFORMATION PER SERVING

Calories	379	Saturated Fat (g)	7
Protein (g)	22	Dietary Fiber (g)	2
Carbohydrate (g)	34	Cholesterol (mg)	93
Fat (g)	17	Sodium (mg)	561
Cal. from Fat (%)	41		

Diabetic Exchanges: 2 lean meat, 2 starch, 0.5 skim milk, 2 fat

CHEESY SHRIMP RICE CASSEROLE

A palate pleasing plain recipe.

1 cup dry brown or wild rice
2 cups water
2 pounds cooked medium
   shrimp, peeled
Salt and pepper to taste

6 ounces light pasteurized
   processed cheese spread
½ cup skim milk
Bread crumbs

Preheat oven to 350 degrees. Cook the rice in the water according to package directions. Set aside. Combine the shrimp, salt and pepper, and the cooked rice. Heat the cheese and milk together in the microwave or in a small pan over medium-low heat until melted, and mix with the rice mixture. Transfer to a 2-quart casserole dish, sprinkle with bread crumbs, and bake for 15 minutes or until well heated.

Makes 6 to 8 servings

Doc's Notes:
A single salad and this casserole is a complete meal. For sore mouth, finely chop shrimp.

NUTRITIONAL INFORMATION PER SERVING

Calories	250	Saturated Fat (g)	2
Protein (g)	30	Dietary Fiber (g)	1
Carbohydrate (g)	21	Cholesterol (mg)	230
Fat (g)	4	Sodium (mg)	601
Cal. from Fat (%)	15		

Diabetic Exchanges: 5 very lean meat, 1.5 starch

CHICKEN POT PIE

I always get excited when I prepare this recipe, because it looks just as perfect as the commercially prepared ones but it tastes so much better! Use leftover chicken.

1 cup diced carrot	2 cups diced cooked skinless, boneless chicken breasts
1 cup sliced mushrooms	½ teaspoon pepper, optional
½ cup chopped celery	½ teaspoon dried thyme leaves
½ cup frozen peas, thawed	1 cup self-rising flour
¼ cup finely chopped onion	1 tablespoon canola oil
¼ cup all-purpose flour	½ cup skim milk
1 (12-ounce) can evaporated skimmed milk	

Preheat oven to 450 degrees. Coat a large skillet with nonstick cooking spray and place over medium-high heat. Add the carrots, mushrooms, celery, peas, and onion and sauté 5 minutes, or until the vegetables are tender. Stir in the all-purpose flour. Gradually add the evaporated milk, stirring until the mixture thickens. Stir in the chicken, pepper, and thyme. Transfer the mixture into a 9-inch pie plate coated with nonstick cooking spray. Place the self-rising flour in a small bowl; cut in the oil with a pastry blender or two knives until the mixture is crumbly. Gradually add milk, stirring just until the ingredients are moistened. Drop the dough evenly by spoonfuls onto the chicken mixture. Bake, uncovered, for 15 to 20 minutes, or until the crust is golden.

Makes 6 servings

Doc's Notes:

This is a complete meal. Carrots provide beta carotene and fiber while the mushrooms are filled with B vitamins, copper, and other minerals. Celery is rich in Vitamin C and folacin.

NUTRITIONAL INFORMATION PER SERVING

Calories	273	Saturated Fat (g)	1
Protein (g)	24	Dietary Fiber (g)	2
Carbohydrate (g)	33	Cholesterol (mg)	42
Fat (g)	5	Sodium (mg)	414
Cal. from Fat (%)	15		

Diabetic Exchanges: 2 very lean meat, 1.5 starch, 0.5 skim milk, 1 vegetable

CHICKEN PICCATA

This recipe continually gets rave reviews in my house. Simple elegance.

½ cup all-purpose flour
Salt and pepper to taste
1 teaspoon dried oregano
   leaves
2 pounds boneless skinless
   chicken breasts
3 tablespoons olive oil

2 cups canned fat-free
   chicken broth
1 teaspoon minced garlic
¼ cup lemon juice
2 tablespoons chopped
   parsley, optional

In a small bowl, combine flour, salt and pepper, and oregano. Coat each chicken piece with mixture; set aside. In a skillet coated with nonstick cooking spray, heat oil and cook chicken breasts on each side until golden brown over medium-high heat. Remove chicken from pan as needed to brown all pieces. Add chicken broth, garlic, and lemon juice to pan, scraping sides of pan. Return chicken to pan and bring to a boil. Reduce heat, cover, and simmer for 10 to 15 minutes or until chicken is done. Sprinkle with parsley, if not neutropenic, and serve.

Makes 6 to 8 servings

Doc's Notes:
Don't use fresh parsley if neutropenic.

NUTRITIONAL INFORMATION PER SERVING

Calories 205
Protein (g) 28
Carbohydrate (g) 7
Fat (g) 7
Cal. from Fat (%) 30

Saturated Fat (g) 1
Dietary Fiber (g) 0
Cholesterol (mg) 66
Sodium (mg) 229

Diabetic Exchanges: 3 very lean meat, 0.5 starch, 1 fat

VERY GOOD VEAL

Veal is a nice variation from time to time.

1½ pounds thinly sliced veal (scaloppini)
¼ cup all-purpose flour
1 tablespoon paprika
Salt and pepper to taste
1 tablespoon margarine
½ teaspoon minced garlic
¼ cup water
1 cup nonfat plain yogurt
1 teaspoon dried basil leaves
1 tablespoon lemon juice
½ teaspoon dried rosemary
¼ cup Marsala wine, optional

Cut the veal into bite-size pieces. Combine the flour, paprika, and salt and pepper in a plastic zip-top bag. Drop the veal into the bag and shake to coat well. In a large skillet, melt the margarine and add the veal pieces and garlic. Sauté over a medium high heat about 3 minutes, turning frequently, until the veal is browned. Add the water, scraping the bottom of the skillet. Lower the heat and stir in the yogurt, one spoonful at a time until well blended. Mix in the basil, lemon juice, rosemary, and Marsala wine. Heat thoroughly, about 5 minutes, but do not boil.

Makes 6 servings

Doc's Notes:

This is easy to prepare and is a good meal for a special occasion such as the night before your last chemotherapy treatment.

NUTRITIONAL INFORMATION PER SERVING

Calories	192	Saturated Fat (g)	2
Protein (g)	25	Dietary Fiber (g)	1
Carbohydrate (g)	8	Cholesterol (mg)	103
Fat (g)	6	Sodium (mg)	164
Cal. from Fat (%)	28		

Diabetic Exchanges: 3 lean meat, 0.5 starch

HOT FRUIT COMPOTE

Open cans and you have a tasty fruit dish.
Great substitute for fresh fruit.

2 bananas, sliced	1 (16½-ounce) can pitted
1 tablespoon lemon juice	Bing cherries, drained
1 (29-ounce) can "lite" sliced	1 (20-ounce) can pineapple
peaches, drained	chunks in its own juice,
1 (16-ounce) can "lite" pear	drained
halves, drained and sliced	¼ cup cornstarch
1 (16-ounce) can "lite"	1 cup light brown sugar
apricot halves, drained	½ teaspoon curry
and sliced	6 tablespoons margarine,
	melted

Preheat oven to 350 degrees. Sprinkle bananas with lemon juice. Mix peaches, pears, apricots, cherries, and pineapple with bananas. Transfer to a 3-quart glass baking dish. In small bowl, combine cornstarch, brown sugar, and curry. Sprinkle over fruit. Drizzle margarine over top of dish. Bake, covered, for 30 minutes. Uncover, and bake for another 15 minutes or until bubbly.

Makes 12 to 15 servings

Doc's Notes:
This is a great source of fruit when you are neutropenic and cannot have fresh fruit. The fruits provide Vitamins A and C and beta carotene.

NUTRITIONAL INFORMATION PER SERVING

Calories	188	Saturated Fat (g)	1
Protein (g)	1	Dietary Fiber (g)	2
Carbohydrate (g)	38	Cholesterol (mg)	0
Fat (g)	5	Sodium (mg)	66
Cal. from Fat (%)	21		

Diabetic Exchanges: 1.5 fruit, 1 other carb., 1 fat

HEAVENLY YAM DELIGHT

A sweet potato version of a favorite layered dessert.
The perfect treat to make when you're in a hurry,
wonderful! If you enjoy pumpkin, you'll love this treat.

1   cup all-purpose flour
¼   cup plus ⅔ cup
    confectioners' sugar,
    divided
⅓   cup chopped pecans
6   tablespoons margarine,
    softened
1   (8-ounce) package fat-free
    cream cheese

1   (8-ounce) container fat-free
    frozen whipped topping,
    thawed, divided
1   (29-ounce) can sweet
    potatoes (yams), drained
½   teaspoon ground cinnamon
¼   cup granulated sugar

Preheat oven to 350 degrees. In a large bowl, combine flour, ¼ cup confectioners' sugar, pecans, and margarine. Press into bottom of 13x9x2-inch baking pan. Bake 20 minutes. Set aside to cool. In a mixing bowl, mix cream cheese and remaining ⅔ cup confectioners' sugar until creamy. Fold in ¾ cup whipped topping. Spread cream cheese mixture over cooled crust. In a mixing bowl, beat sweet potatoes, cinnamon, and granulated sugar until smooth. Spread over cream cheese mixture. Top with remaining whipped topping. Refrigerate.

Makes 16 servings

Doc's Notes:
When your white blood cell count is low, this will surely give you a lift. Remember your blood counts will normally only stay down for 4 to 7 days.

NUTRITIONAL INFORMATION PER SERVING

Calories	205	Saturated Fat (g)	1
Protein (g)	4	Dietary Fiber (g)	2
Carbohydrate (g)	33	Cholesterol (mg)	1
Fat (g)	6	Sodium (mg)	143
Cal. from Fat (%)	28		

Diabetic Exchanges: 1 starch, 1 other carb., 1 fat

MOCHA CAPPUCCINO PUDDING PIE

This incredibly wonderful pie is very soothing to taste.
For Deluxe Chocolate Pie, leave out the coffee.

1   (4-serving) package instant
      chocolate pudding
2   teaspoons coffee granules
1   cup skim milk
1   cup fat-free vanilla ice cream

1   cup fat-free frozen
      whipped topping, thawed
1   prepared reduced-fat
      graham cracker crust

Combine pudding mix, coffee granules, milk, and ice cream. Beat 2 minutes or until creamy. Fold in whipped topping. Transfer to prepared pie crust. Freeze 30 minutes or longer before serving. Can also be made as a parfait.

Makes 8 servings

Doc's Notes:

This is a great snack or use it as a dessert. Substitute a vanilla nutritional energy drink supplement for the skim milk to add vitamins, minerals, and calories.

NUTRITIONAL INFORMATION PER SERVING

Calories	203	Saturated Fat (g)	1
Protein (g)	3	Dietary Fiber (g)	1
Carbohydrate (g)	39	Cholesterol (mg)	1
Fat (g)	3	Sodium (mg)	332
Cal. from Fat (%)	15		

Diabetic Exchanges: 1.5 starch, 1 other carb., 0.5 fat

BAKED PEACH DELIGHT

This will intrigue your guests. A great substitute for fresh fruit.
Adjust recipe according to number of peach halves in the can.

1   (16-ounce) can peach   5   teaspoons light brown
    halves, drained (5 halves)   sugar
5   tablespoons reduced-fat
    peanut butter

Preheat oven to 350 degrees. Place peach halves in a baking dish, pit-side up. Spread 1 tablespoon peanut butter on each peach half and sprinkle each with 1 teaspoon brown sugar. Bake until peanut butter and brown sugar melt, about 5 to 10 minutes.

Makes 5 servings

Doc's Notes:
Peaches provide the Vitamin C while the peanut butter adds protein to this dish.

NUTRITIONAL INFORMATION PER SERVING

Calories	135	Saturated Fat (g)	1
Protein (g)	5	Dietary Fiber (g)	2
Carbohydrate (g)	20	Cholesterol (mg)	0
Fat (g)	5	Sodium (mg)	94
Cal. from Fat (%)	33		

Diabetic Exchanges: 0.5 very lean meat, 1 fruit, 0.5 other carb., 1 fat

Neutropenia

PEACH SMOOTHIE

Serve with gingersnaps or honey graham crackers.

2   cups canned sliced peaches, drained
1   (12-ounce) can peach nectar
1   cup nonfat vanilla yogurt
½   teaspoon almond extract, optional
1   cup chopped ice

In a food processor or blender, combine all ingredients and blend until mixture is smooth and frothy.

Makes two (1-cup) servings

Doc's Notes:

For extra vitamins and calories, use a nutritional energy drink supplement instead of the yogurt.

NUTRITIONAL INFORMATION PER SERVING

Calories	326	Saturated Fat (g)	0
Protein (g)	8	Dietary Fiber (g)	4
Carbohydrate (g)	77	Cholesterol (mg)	0
Fat (g)	0	Sodium (mg)	107
Cal. from Fat (%)	0		

Diabetic Exchanges: 3 fruit, 1 skim milk, 1 other carb.

PEACH WEIGHT GAIN SHAKE

Peaches and almond disguise the taste of the supplement.

1   (12-ounce) can vanilla nutritional energy drink supplement
½   teaspoon almond extract
1   (15-ounce) can sliced peaches in syrup, drained

Pour supplement, extract, and peaches into a blender. Blend and chill or serve over ice.

Makes 2 servings

Doc's Notes:

Remember to have an adequate number of calories per day.

NUTRITIONAL INFORMATION PER SERVING

Calories	298	Saturated Fat (g)	0
Protein (g)	8	Dietary Fiber (g)	2
Carbohydrate (g)	61	Cholesterol (mg)	0
Fat (g)	3	Sodium (mg)	106
Cal. from Fat (%)	9		

Diabetic Exchanges: 2 starch, 2 fruit

BASIC WEIGHT GAIN SHAKE

Also great for sore mouth. Add frozen banana if desired.

½ cup chocolate nutritional
   energy drink supplement,
   chilled

½ cup reduced-fat vanilla ice
   cream

Place supplement and ice cream in a blender and blend until well mixed.
Pour into a large glass and serve.

Makes 1 serving

Doc's Notes:
Great supplement for extra calories as it includes all the vitamins
and nutrients you need to survive.

NUTRITIONAL INFORMATION PER SERVING

Calories	228	Saturated Fat (g)	1
Protein (g)	8	Dietary Fiber (g)	1
Carbohydrate (g)	39	Cholesterol (mg)	5
Fat (g)	4	Sodium (mg)	109
Cal. from Fat (%)	16		

*Diabetic Exchanges: 0.5 very lean meat, 1.5 starch, 1 other carb.,
0.5 fat*

HOT COCOA DRINK SUPPLEMENT

*Packages of cocoa mix turn these drinks into
chocolate delights. Coffee lovers, stir in ½ teaspoon
instant coffee. For Cocoa Smoothie, add cocoa mix to
½ cup chilled chocolate nutritional energy drink supplement
and ½ cup ice cubes in a blender and blend until smooth.*

1   **(8-ounce) can nutritional**   1   **package hot cocoa mix**
      energy drink supplement

Pour supplement into a large microwave-safe mug and microwave until very hot. Gradually stir in the cocoa mix until well blended.

Makes 1 serving

Doc's Notes:

A great drink on cold mornings for extra calories, vitamins, and minerals.

NUTRITIONAL INFORMATION PER SERVING

Calories	348	Saturated Fat (g)	0
Protein (g)	11	Dietary Fiber (g)	1
Carbohydrate (g)	65	Cholesterol (mg)	2
Fat (g)	5	Sodium (mg)	230
Cal. from Fat (%)	13		

Diabetic Exchanges: 0.5 very lean meat, 3 starch, 1.5 other carb.

DIARRHEA

◈ *Will it ever stop?*
◈ *Should I stop eating and drinking altogether?*
◈ *What should I eat and drink?*
◈ *Is it alright to take Immodium, Lomotil or Pepto Bismol?*
◈ *My rectum is sore, what can I do? (Don't panic, help is on the way!)*

Diarrhea can follow certain chemotherapy or radiation treatments. This can be a problem with certain drugs such as 5-FU, CPT-11 and antibiotics. If the diarrhea starts, the first thing to do is to stop all intake of high fiber foods, stool softeners or laxatives. Follow your doctors' instructions with regards to Lomotil, Immodium, or Pepto Bismol. Start clear liquids after fasting two to four hours. Force fluids up to eight to ten glasses per day. Water, clear soup, broth, flat soda or a sports drink are excellent fluids to replace those lost by diarrhea. Avoid dairy products since they tend to make diarrhea worse. Hot and cold beverages, alcohol, coffee and cigarettes tend to aggravate diarrhea.

Bananas, rice, applesauce and toast are good foods to begin eating following a decrease in your diarrhea. Once you are tolerating these foods, progress to bland low fiber foods, such as chicken without the skin, scrambled eggs, and canned or cooked fruits without skins. Crackers, pasta without sauce, white bread or gelatins are good choices. Try to avoid foods high in fiber, such as grains, raw vegetables, whole wheat, raw fruit, oatmeal and brown rice.

Nuts, beans and milk products may worsen the diarrhea. Any high fat food should be avoided. Try to avoid caffeine and hot or spicy foods. Once your diarrhea has subsided, you can adjust your diet accordingly. Foods low in fiber and fat are helpful in decreasing your diarrhea.

If your rectum becomes red or sore, use a commercial wet towel without alcohol and avoid dry toilet paper. Desitin or a combination of Aquaphor and Questran in a 9 to 1 ratio, will act as a protective barrier to your perirectal area. Ask your physician to prescribe these medications.

If your diarrhea continues without relief for greater than twenty-four hours, please notify your physician. I hope the recipes and suggestions that follow will help to get you regulated and eating healthy again.

Points to Remember

- Eat chicken soup or bouillon cubes dissolved in water.
- Eat bland, high-protein foods.
- Eat smaller mini meals throughout the day to see what you can tolerate.
- Eat high-calorie, low-fiber foods.
- Avoid citrus juices and carbonated beverages. An alternative to carbonated drinks is mineral water with a splash of fruit juices, which is both bubbly and tasty.
- Avoid raw vegetables and fruits, and high fiber foods, nuts, onions, garlic, and gaseous vegetables.
- Avoid spicy foods.
- Avoid greasy, fatty, or fried foods.
- Drink beverages frequently, in small amounts, and at room temperatures.
- Limit caffeine intake.
- Choose low fiber light foods like fish, chicken, eggs, bananas, potatoes, low fiber cereals, crackers, refined bread and flour products. Crackers with peanut butter or cheese sometimes works.
- Do minimal activity after meals.
- Ginger can be soothing to the stomach: ginger snaps, ginger candy

Some Foods to Include

- Toast, crackers or pretzels
- Flavored gelatin
- Applesauce
- Skinless chicken
- Clear liquids
- Bananas
- Rice
- Plums, peaches, watermelon, cantaloupe
- Squash, eggplant

MENUS
Foods to eat to ease diarrhea

Breakfast

Scrambled Eggs
Grits
Easy Banana Bread (p. 80)

Baked French Toast (p. 26)

Cinnamon Rolls without Raisins and Pecans (p. 23)

Lunch

Quick Chicken Pasta (p. 86)
Applesauce
Rolls

Plain Turkey Sandwich

Dinner

Oven Fried Parmesan Chicken (p. 85)
Baked Potato
Banana Pudding (p. 89)

Chicken Scampi (p. 87)
Creamy Squash Casserole (p. 82)
Pasta
Mocha Meringue Mounds (p. 172)

Roasted Turkey Breast (p. 84)
Pasta Toss
Coffee Cake (p. 169)

Snacks

Banana Bread (p. 174)

Cinnamon Quick Bread (p. 156)

Banana Puff (p. 81)

Diarrhea

EASY BANANA BREAD

This is a short cut banana bread, thanks to the biscuit mix.

1 (8-ounce) package light cream cheese, softened	1 large egg, beaten
	2 large egg whites
1 cup sugar	2 cups biscuit baking mix
3 medium bananas, mashed	½ teaspoon ground cinnamon

Preheat oven to 350 degrees. Coat a 9x5x3-inch loaf pan with non-stick cooking spray. In a mixing bowl, cream together the cream cheese and sugar until light. Beat in the bananas, egg, and egg whites. Stir in the biscuit mix and cinnamon until just blended. Turn into the prepared loaf pan. Bake for 45 minutes to 1 hour, until a toothpick inserted in the center comes out clean. Cool in the pan 15 minutes.

Makes 16 slices

Doc's Notes:

Bananas are a great source of potassium. They are easily digested by virtually everyone. The high carbohydrate content makes bananas the snack of choice for endurance athletes.

NUTRITIONAL INFORMATION PER SERVING

Calories	168	Saturated Fat (g)	2
Protein (g)	3	Dietary Fiber (g)	1
Carbohydrate (g)	28	Cholesterol (mg)	20
Fat (g)	5	Sodium (mg)	267
Cal. from Fat (%)	26		

Diabetic Exchanges: 0.5 starch, 0.5 fruit, 1 other carb., 0.5 fat

BANANA PUFF

A light tasty meal for breakfast or any time of day.

2   eggs, separated
¼   cup sugar
1   cup nonfat plain yogurt
2   tablespoons margarine,
      melted
1   teaspoon vanilla extract

½   teaspoon imitation butter
      flavoring
¾   cup all-purpose flour
2   teaspoons baking powder
1   teaspoon baking soda
¼   teaspoon ground cinnamon
1   banana, diced

Preheat oven to 400 degrees. In a mixing bowl, beat egg yolks, sugar, yogurt, and margarine until blended. Add flavorings. Combine dry ingredients, and beat into egg mixture until all ingredients are moistened. In another bowl, beat egg whites until stiff. Carefully fold into batter. Fold in bananas. Spread batter into a 9-inch round cake pan coated with nonstick cooking spray. Bake for 20 to 25 minutes. Serve immediately.

Makes 8 servings

NUTRITIONAL INFORMATION PER SERVING

Calories	145	Saturated Fat (g)	1
Protein (g)	5	Dietary Fiber (g)	1
Carbohydrate (g)	22	Cholesterol (mg)	54
Fat (g)	4	Sodium (mg)	352
Cal. from Fat (%)	27		

Diabetic Exchanges: 0.5 starch, 0.5 fruit, 0.5 other carb., 1 fat

CREAMY SQUASH CASSEROLE

Here's another way to turn squash into an incredible dish.
Make ahead and refrigerate; pop into a cold oven to bake.

2   pounds yellow squash
    (about 8), sliced
1   cup nonfat plain yogurt
Salt and pepper to taste
½   teaspoon dried basil leaves
½   cup dry bread crumbs

¼   cup shredded reduced-fat
    sharp Cheddar cheese,
    optional
1   tablespoon margarine,
    melted
½   teaspoon paprika

Preheat oven to 350 degrees. Coat a 1½-quart casserole dish with non-stick cooking spray. Boil the squash in a saucepan in a small amount of water over a medium to high heat until tender, about 5 minutes. Drain well. Combine the squash with yogurt, salt and pepper, and basil in a mixing bowl. Pour into the casserole dish. Combine the bread crumbs, Cheddar cheese, margarine, and paprika. Sprinkle over the squash mixture. Bake for 20 minutes.

Makes 6 to 8 servings

Doc's Notes:
Squash is low in fiber so here's a great way to include a veggie at this time.

NUTRITIONAL INFORMATION PER SERVING

Calories 84
Protein (g) 4
Carbohydrate (g) 13
Fat (g) 2
Cal. from Fat (%) 22
Saturated Fat (g) 0

Dietary Fiber (g) 3
Cholesterol (mg) 1
Sodium (mg) 101

Diabetic Exchanges: 0.5 starch,

1 vegetable

PASTA TOSS

Use whatever pasta that is in your pantry.

1 (16-ounce) package pasta
2 tablespoons olive oil
1 cup chopped tomato
1 tablespoon minced garlic
1 teaspoon dried basil leaves

1 cup coarsely chopped
  green onions (scallions)
⅓ cup grated Parmesan
  cheese

Prepare the pasta according to package directions; drain and set aside. In a large skillet, heat the olive oil and sauté tomato and garlic for 1 minute. Add the basil and green onions and pasta. Toss with the Parmesan cheese.

Makes 8 servings

Doc's Notes:
Depending on how you feel, adjust the amount of tomatoes and green onions.

NUTRITIONAL INFORMATION PER SERVING

Calories	270	Saturated Fat (g)	1
Protein (g)	10	Dietary Fiber (g)	2
Carbohydrate (g)	45	Cholesterol (mg)	3
Fat (g)	6	Sodium (mg)	86
Cal. from Fat (%)	19		

Diabetic Exchanges: 3 starch, 1 fat

ROASTED TURKEY BREAST

Easy and herbs enhance a plain turkey breast.

1	(3-pound) fresh turkey breast	1	teaspoon dried thyme leaves
½	cup canned fat-free chicken broth	1	teaspoon dried oregano leaves
1	tablespoon dried rosemary	¼	teaspoon black pepper
1	teaspoon garlic powder		

Preheat oven to 375 degrees. Rinse the breast and pat dry. Place in a shallow baking dish. Add the broth and enough water to come up to ¼ inch in the dish. Sprinkle the rosemary, garlic powder, thyme, oregano, and pepper all over turkey. Bake for 1 to 1½ hours or until the internal temperature is 170 degrees on a meat thermometer. Remove skin before serving.

Makes 8 servings

Doc's Notes:
Light and easy on the stomach when you have had problems with diarrhea.

NUTRITIONAL INFORMATION PER SERVING

Calories	150	Saturated Fat (g)	0
Protein (g)	33	Dietary Fiber (g)	0
Carbohydrate (g)	1	Cholesterol (mg)	89
Fat (g)	1	Sodium (mg)	119
Cal. from Fat (%)	6		

Diabetic Exchanges: 4 very lean meat

OVEN FRIED PARMESAN CHICKEN

Easy, tasty and will fulfill your urge for old-fashioned fried chicken. Cut recipe in half to prepare less. This chicken is good the next day on a sandwich.

¾ cup nonfat plain yogurt
¼ cup lemon juice
1½ tablespoons Dijon mustard
3 cloves garlic, minced
½ teaspoon dried oregano leaves

10 boneless, skinless chicken breasts
2 tablespoons margarine, melted

Combine all ingredients except margarine. Marinate, covered, 2 hours or overnight in refrigerator. Preheat oven to 350 degrees. Drain chicken and coat with Bread Crumb Coating (recipe follows). Place on a baking sheet coated with nonstick cooking spray and chill for 1 hour (if time permits). Drizzle chicken with margarine. Bake for 45 minutes to 1 hour or until tender and golden brown.

Bread Crumb Coating
2 cups dry bread crumbs or Italian bread crumbs
¼ cup grated Parmesan cheese

Combine all coating ingredients in shallow bowl.

Makes 10 servings

NUTRITIONAL INFORMATION PER SERVING

Calories	246	Saturated Fat (g)	2
Protein (g)	30	Dietary Fiber (g)	1
Carbohydrate (g)	16	Cholesterol (mg)	68
Fat (g)	6	Sodium (mg)	347
Cal. from Fat (%)	21		

Diabetic Exchanges: 3 lean meat, 1 starch

QUICK CHICKEN PASTA

When feeling better, this dish is quick to prepare and quick to disappear from the plate. If you can't tolerate mushrooms, onion or tomato, leave out for a plainer version, until you feel better.

1 tablespoon olive oil	½ cup chopped red onion, optional
2 pounds boneless skinless chicken breasts, cut into strips	1 tablespoon dried basil leaves
Salt and pepper to taste	⅓ cup canned fat-free chicken broth
1 large tomato, diced	1 (8-ounce) package angel hair (capellini) pasta
1 cup sliced mushrooms	¼ cup grated Romano cheese
1 teaspoon minced garlic	

In a large pan coated with nonstick cooking spray, heat the olive oil and sauté the chicken until almost done, about 4 minutes. Season with salt and pepper. Add the tomato, mushrooms, garlic, onion, and basil, stirring for 5 minutes or until veggies are tender. Add the chicken broth, cooking until heated through. Meanwhile, cook the pasta according to package directions, omitting any oil and salt. Drain and set aside. When the chicken is done, toss with the pasta and Romano cheese.

Makes 4 servings

Doc's Notes:
Leaving out the onions and tomatoes will make this dish an excellent meal if you have diarrhea.

NUTRITIONAL INFORMATION PER SERVING

Calories	543	Saturated Fat (g)	2
Protein (g)	63	Dietary Fiber (g)	3
Carbohydrate (g)	49	Cholesterol (mg)	138
Fat (g)	9	Sodium (mg)	284
Cal. from Fat (%)	15		

Diabetic Exchanges: 7 very lean meat, 3 starch, 1 vegetable

CHICKEN SCAMPI

Cut the chicken into strips and toss with pasta and you have a super combination. I have always loved shrimp scampi and now you can enjoy the same flavor with chicken.

2 pounds boneless, skinless chicken breasts	¼ teaspoon garlic powder
1 tablespoon olive oil	Salt and pepper to taste
2 tablespoons grated Parmesan cheese	1 tablespoon dried oregano leaves
1 tablespoon dried parsley flakes	3 tablespoons lemon juice
	2 tablespoons Worcestershire sauce

Combine all the ingredients in a shallow bowl. Marinate, covered, in the refrigerator for several hours or overnight. Preheat the broiler. Remove the chicken from the marinade and place in a single layer in a shallow baking dish or broiling pan. Broil 8 inches from the heat, turning once, until the chicken is done, about 15 minutes.

Makes 6 servings

Doc's Notes:

You will find this dish to be light and easy on your gastrointestinal tract. Boiled plain pasta and dry toast is a good meal to try once your diarrhea is decreasing.

NUTRITIONAL INFORMATION PER SERVING

Calories 176	Saturated Fat (g) 1
Protein (g) 35	Dietary Fiber (g) 0
Carbohydrate (g) 1	Cholesterol (mg) 88
Fat (g) 3	Sodium (mg) 146
Cal. from Fat (%) 14	

Diabetic Exchanges: 4 very lean meat

SHRIMP AND SQUASH SCAMPI

Shrimp and squash pair to make a superb meal.

1   (8-ounce) package small pasta or orzo
2   tablespoons olive oil
1   pound zucchini, halved lengthwise and sliced
1   pound yellow squash, halved lengthwise and sliced
1   pound raw medium shrimp, peeled
1   tablespoon minced garlic
¾   cup clam juice or chicken broth
2   tablespoons lemon juice
2   tablespoons chopped parsley
¼   cup grated Parmesan cheese, optional

Cook the pasta according to package directions. Drain; set aside. Meanwhile, in a large skillet, heat the olive oil over a medium high heat and stir fry the zucchini and squash until crisp tender, about 5 minutes. Add the shrimp and continue cooking for another 5 minutes or until the shrimp are almost done. Add the garlic, clam juice, and lemon juice, cooking until the shrimp are done, about 3 to 5 minutes. Add the parsley, pasta, and Parmesan cheese, tossing to mix well.

Makes 4 servings

Doc's Notes:
The squash and zucchini are actually low in fiber. This is a good choice if you are not having severe diarrhea.

NUTRITIONAL INFORMATION PER SERVING

Calories	412	Saturated Fat (g)	3
Protein (g)	27	Dietary Fiber (g)	5
Carbohydrate (g)	52	Cholesterol (mg)	140
Fat (g)	11	Sodium (mg)	582
Cal. from Fat (%)	23		

Diabetic Exchanges: 2 very lean meat, 3 starch, 2 vegetable, 1 fat

BANANA PUDDING

Layer with vanilla wafers and bananas
for an old-fashioned banana pudding.

1   (4-serving) package instant   2   cups skim milk
    banana pudding mix   2   bananas, diced

In a mixing bowl, mix banana pudding and milk with a whisk for 2 minutes. Fold cut up bananas into pudding. For pudding, transfer to cups and refrigerate.

Makes 4 servings

Doc's Notes:

For extra calories, substitute vanilla nutritional energy drink supplement for skim milk. It's a great way to sneak extra vitamins and calories into your diet. No bananas if your blood counts are low.

NUTRITIONAL INFORMATION PER SERVING

Calories 188   Saturated Fat (g) 0
Protein (g) 5   Dietary Fiber (g) 1
Carbohydrate (g) 43   Cholesterol (mg) 2
Fat (g) 1   Sodium (mg) 435
Cal. from Fat (%) 3

Diabetic Exchanges: 0.5 skim milk, 1 fruit, 1.5 other carb.

GLAZED BANANAS

*Serve over frozen vanilla yogurt at a later date
and you will have a sensational simple dessert.*

Diarrhea

2	tablespoons margarine	¼	cup orange juice
¼	cup light brown sugar	3	firm bananas, peeled, split
⅛	teaspoon ground cinnamon		lengthwise and halved

In pan, heat margarine, brown sugar, cinnamon, and orange juice until bubbly. Add banana slices and cook for 5 minutes, turning as needed. Serve immediately.

Makes 6 servings

Doc's Notes:

This can be eaten with or without the yogurt. Great food if diarrhea is a problem. Bananas help to replace the potassium lost with the diarrhea.

NUTRITIONAL INFORMATION PER SERVING

Calories	127	Saturated Fat (g)	1
Protein (g)	1	Dietary Fiber (g)	2
Carbohydrate (g)	24	Cholesterol (mg)	0
Fat (g)	4	Sodium (mg)	49
Cal. from Fat (%)....................	27		

Diabetic Exchanges: 1 fruit, 0.5 other carb., 1 fat

CONSTIPATION

❖ How often do I need to have a bowel movement?
❖ Should I take a stool softener?
❖ Why am I constipated when I have never had this problem before?
❖ Are there any foods that will aid in the relief of my constipation?

Constipation can be a problem at any time during your treatment. Certain drugs such as pain medicines and chemotherapy, namely Vincristine, are commonly associated with constipation. Normally, you need to have a bowel movement every forty-eight to seventy-two hours. This will vary among people. You should only be concerned if you notice a difference from your normal routine.

Stool softeners such as Colace, Surfak, and Senokot are very helpful. Again, six to eight glasses of water is mandatory. Bulk forming agents such as Fibercon, Citrucel, or Metamucil will aid your constipation immensely. Laxatives including Milk of Magnesia, Ducolax, Lactulose, Mineral Oil, Magnesium Citrate, in addition to water and a stool softener or bulk forming agent, will alleviate your constipation.

Constipation will decrease your appetite and generally make you feel bad. Foods high in fiber, such as bran, should be a part of your everyday diet. Muffins made with prune juice instead of water can aid the problem. Fruit salads, vegetable dishes, beans, grains, bread, fruit drinks, figs, raisins, apples, brown rice, pudding and stewed prunes are a few foods which can help keep you regular. If a healthy diet, stool softeners, and laxatives fail, contact your physician. You should not go over seventy-two hours without a bowel movement. The following foods and recipes should really be helpful for you.

Points to Remember

- Drink lots and lots of fluid. Try drinking a warm beverage.
- Increase intake of high fiber foods.
- Try adding shredded veggies into other casseroles or recipes.
- Add oat or wheat bran to casseroles.
- Try adding 2 tablespoons wheat bran a day to your diet…drink water.
- Bran such as wheat bran may be added to baked goods or casseroles. By consuming 2 tablespoons of wheat bran, your stools will be softer and easier to pass. Remember when you increase bran intake, increase your water intake also.
- Eat more vegetables; raw or cooked; broccoli, carrots, and celery.
- Try eating whole grain cereals and breads.
- Do light exercise after eating.
- Try drinking a hot beverage 30 minutes before the usual time for a bowel movement.

MENUS
Foods to eat to ease constipation

Breakfast
Sweet Potato Pancakes with Apple Walnut Topping (p. 96)

Honey Bran Prune Muffins (p. 125)
Egg of choice
Orange Juice

Spinach Layered Dish (p. 175)
Banana Bran Muffins (p. 126)
Fresh Fruit

Lunch
Mushroom Barley Soup (p. 99)
Chicken Salad (p. 106)
Oatmeal Chocolate Cake (p. 130)

Sweet Potato and Apple Soup (p. 104)
Tuna Salad (p. 38)
Whole Wheat Toast

White Bean and Tortellini Soup (p. 98)

Salad Medley:
Black Bean and Corn Salad (p. 111)
Waldorf Salad (p. 105)
Tuna Pasta Salad (p. 109)
Zucchini Oatmeal Raisin Muffins (p. 123)

Strawberry Raspberry Soup (p. 95)
Yam Veggie Wraps (p. 117)

Dinner
Comfort Food:
Meat Loaf (p. 121)
Basic Broccoli (p. 113)
Creamed Double Potatoes (p. 144)
Peach Crumble (p. 131)

One Dish Meals Suggestions:
Vegetable Lasagna (p. 118)
Red Beans and Rice (p. 119)
Southwestern Pasta (p. 120)
Chicken Tortilla Soup (p. 180)

Cream of Spinach Soup (p. 179)
Chicken with Bean Sauce (p. 221)
Baked Corn Casserole (p. 113)

Tropical Green Salad (p. 210)
Shrimp and Wild Rice Salad (p. 108)

Quick Veggie Soup (p. 100)
Italian Spinach Pie (p. 167)

Snacks
Avocado Soup (p. 140)

Granola (p. 94)

Strawberry Salsa (p. 159)

Cereal Mixture (p. 153)

Strawberry Slush (p. 152)

Couscous Salad (p. 204)

GRANOLA

This crunchy mixture makes a great snack or just sprinkle it on fruit, yogurt or ice cream. Add whatever fruit combos you enjoy and throw in some nuts, if desired.

4 cups old-fashioned oatmeal	½ cup pumpkin seeds
½ cup wheat bran	⅔ cup honey
2 tablespoons nonfat dry milk	2 tablespoons molasses
	½ cup dried cranberries
1 teaspoon ground cinnamon	1 cup dried mixed fruit bits
½ cup sunflower seeds	

Preheat oven to 300 degrees. Line a baking sheet with heavy foil to make clean up a snap. Mix together the oatmeal, bran, dry milk, cinnamon, sunflower and pumpkin seed and spread on the lined pan. In a small bowl, mix together the honey and molasses. Pour the honey mixture over the cereal, stirring and tossing until well coated. Place in the oven for 30 to 35 minutes, stirring every 15 minutes, and cooking until mixture is golden brown. Let cool and toss with the cranberries and dried mixed fruit.

Makes sixteen (½-cup) servings

Doc's Notes:

Keep a jar of this for nibbles throughout the day. This beats the taste of any laxative. This is truly a great source of fiber. The fiber pulls fluid into the colon, softening the stool and aiding in bowel movements.

NUTRITIONAL INFORMATION PER SERVING

Calories	228	Saturated Fat (g)	1
Protein (g)	7	Dietary Fiber (g)	4
Carbohydrate (g)	39	Cholesterol (mg)	0
Fat (g)	7	Sodium (mg)	10
Cal. from Fat (%)	25		

Diabetic Exchanges: 1 starch, 0.5 fruit, 1 other carb., 1 fat

STRAWBERRY RASPBERRY SOUP

A fabulous berry soup!

1	quart fresh strawberries, halved	¼	cup sugar
3	cups fresh raspberries or 1 (12-ounce) package frozen raspberries, drained	2	tablespoon cornstarch
		1	cup water
		1	tablespoon lemon juice
		¾	cup nonfat plain yogurt
½	cup plus ⅔ cup apple juice, divided	1½	teaspoons powdered sugar
		½	teaspoon vanilla extract

Place the strawberries, raspberries, ½ cup apple juice, and sugar in a saucepan and let stand 15 minutes. Heat over low heat until boiling. Mix together the cornstarch and water, and stir into fruit mixture. Boil over low heat, stirring constantly, until fruits soften and soup is clear and thickened. Remove from heat and stir in the lemon juice. Chill. Before serving add remaining ⅔ cup apple juice to make soup consistency, or more if needed. In a small bowl, combine yogurt, powdered sugar, and vanilla. Serve soup in small bowls and top each with a tablespoon of yogurt mixture.

Makes 12 small servings

Doc's Notes:
High in Vitamin C and potassium as well as a good source of fiber.

NUTRITIONAL INFORMATION PER SERVING

Calories	73	Saturated Fat (g)	0
Protein (g)	2	Dietary Fiber (g)	3
Carbohydrate (g)	17	Cholesterol (mg)	0
Fat (g)	0	Sodium (mg)	13
Cal. from Fat (%)	0		

Diabetic Exchanges: 1 fruit

SWEET POTATO PANCAKES WITH APPLE WALNUT TOPPING

The indulgent Apple Walnut Topping with the Sweet Potato Pancakes makes this a hard combination to beat. Don't let shredding the potatoes scare you away from this delicious dish as potatoes are easily shredded with the shredding blade of the food processor. The Apple Walnut Topping would be a hit over vanilla ice cream

Pancakes

6	cups shredded peeled sweet potatoes (yams)	1	tablespoon honey
¼	cup all-purpose flour	1	large egg
½	teaspoon baking powder	2	large egg whites
⅛	teaspoon ground cinnamon		Apple Walnut Topping (recipe follows)

In a bowl, combine the shredded sweet potatoes, flour, baking powder, cinnamon, honey, egg, and egg whites with a fork until well blended. Heat a nonstick skillet coated with nonstick cooking spray, and drop about 2 tablespoons of batter (about 3 inches each) into hot pan. Flatten slightly with the spatula and cook pancakes over medium heat until golden on both sides. Set cooked pancakes on a plate and continue cooking until all batter is used. Serve with Apple Walnut Topping.

Note: Pancakes may be frozen or made ahead. To reheat, place on baking sheets and bake at 450 degrees for about 7 to 10 minutes or until crisp.

Makes about 18 pancakes

Apple Walnut Topping

½	cup light brown sugar	1	tablespoon orange juice
⅓	cup chopped walnuts	⅛	teaspoon ground cinnamon
2	baking apples, peeled, core and thinly sliced		

In a skillet, add all the ingredients and cook over a medium-high heat, stirring, until the apples are tender and the brown sugar melts to form a syrup.

Doc's Notes:

A new approach to potato pancakes - sweet potatoes contain lots of beta carotene, offering more nutrition than white potatoes.

(see Nutritional Information on next page)

Calories	104	Saturated Fat (g)	0
Protein (g)	2	Dietary Fiber (g)	2
Carbohydrate (g)	22	Cholesterol (mg)	12
Fat (g)	2	Sodium (mg)	40
Cal. from Fat (%)	15		

Diabetic Exchanges: 1 starch, 0.5 other carb.

TROPICAL SALSA

*This light tropical salsa is the perfect compliment
to any fish, pork, or chicken, or serve with chips.*

1   **(8-ounce) can pineapple
    chunks in its own juice,
    drained**
1   **tablespoon lemon juice**
¼   **teaspoon ground ginger**
1½ **tablespoons light brown
    sugar**

1   **(11-ounce) can mandarin
    orange segments, drained
    and coarsely chopped**
2   **green onions (scallions),
    chopped**
1   **teaspoon chopped pickled
    jalapeño peppers, optional**
1   **tablespoon cilantro, optional**

In a medium bowl, coarsely chop the pineapple and add the lemon
juice, ginger, brown sugar, coarsely chopped mandarin oranges, green
onions, jalapeños, and cilantro; set aside. When ready to serve, heat,
or serve at room temperature with your entrée.

Makes 4 servings

Doc's Notes:
If the jalapeño peppers are too hot, just omit them. Great source of
Vitamin C.

Calories	74	Saturated Fat (g)	0
Protein (g)	1	Dietary Fiber (g)	1
Carbohydrate (g)	19	Cholesterol (mg)	0
Fat (g)	0	Sodium (mg)	28
Cal. from Fat (%)	0		

Diabetic Exchanges: 1 fruit, 0.5 other carb.

WHITE BEAN AND TORTELLINI SOUP

For a quick, very tasty soup, try this recipe.

½ cup chopped green bell pepper
½ cup chopped celery
½ teaspoon minced garlic
8 cups canned fat-free chicken broth
1 (6-ounce) package tri-colored tortellini

1 (15-ounce) can great Northern beans, drained and rinsed
1½ cups chopped tomatoes
1 teaspoon dried oregano leaves
1 teaspoon dried basil leaves
Salt and pepper to taste

In a large pot coated with nonstick cooking spray, sauté the green pepper, celery, and garlic until tender, about 5 to 7 minutes. Add chicken broth and bring to a boil. Add tortellini, reduce heat and cook 15 minutes or until tortellini is done. Add beans, tomatoes, oregano, basil, and salt and pepper. Continue cooking 5 minutes longer.

Makes 8 servings

NUTRITIONAL INFORMATION PER SERVING

Calories 127
Protein (g) 9
Carbohydrate (g) 21
Fat (g) 1
Cal. from Fat (%) 9

Saturated Fat (g) 1
Dietary Fiber (g) 4
Cholesterol (mg) 11
Sodium (mg) 788

Diabetic Exchanges: 0.5 very lean meat, 1 starch, 1 vegetable

MUSHROOM BARLEY SOUP

A savory soup that hits the spot on a cool night.
For a fast version, use quick cooking barley.

1	teaspoon minced garlic	1	(8-ounce) can tomato sauce
1	onion, chopped	8	cups beef or vegetable broth
2	carrots, chopped		
½	pound sliced mushrooms	¾	cup medium pearl barley
1	cup shiitake mushrooms, sliced		Salt and pepper to taste

In a large pot coated with nonstick cooking spray, sauté the garlic, onion, carrot, and mushrooms until tender. Add tomato sauce and broth. Bring to a boil and add barley. Reduce heat, cover, and cook for 1 hour or until barley is done. Season to taste. Add more water if needed.

Makes 8 servings

Doc's Notes:

Soup and sandwich are quick and easy when you do not have a ravenous appetite. This provides fiber, B vitamins, copper, and beta carotene.

NUTRITIONAL INFORMATION PER SERVING

Calories	118	Saturated Fat (g)	0
Protein (g)	8	Dietary Fiber (g)	4
Carbohydrate (g)	21	Cholesterol (mg)	0
Fat (g)	0	Sodium (mg)	1174
Cal. from Fat (%)	0		

Diabetic Exchanges: 1 starch, 1.5 vegetable

QUICK VEGGIE SOUP

Any combination of cooked leftover vegetables may
be substituted for the corn and carrots. Try adding some
shredded cabbage to include a great cruciferous veggie.

1 onion, chopped	1 tablespoon Worcestershire
1 teaspoon minced garlic	sauce
1 (16-ounce) can tomato	1 small bay leaf
purée	1 cup sliced carrots
4 cups water	1 (10-ounce) package frozen
Salt and pepper to taste	corn
1 tablespoon light brown	1 (10-ounce) package frozen
sugar	green peas
	⅓ cup rice

In a large pot coated with nonstick cooking spray, sauté onions and garlic until softened, about 7 minutes. Add the tomato purée, water, salt and pepper, brown sugar, Worcestershire sauce, bay leaf, carrots, and corn. Bring to a boil and simmer for about 20 minutes. Add the peas and rice and simmer about 40 to 45 minutes longer or until the rice is done. Remove the bay leaf before serving. Add more water if needed while cooking to keep a soup consistency.

Makes 6 servings

Doc's Notes:
Freeze in small containers for those nights you just do not have the energy to cook. It provides Vitamin A, beta carotene, and fiber.

NUTRITIONAL INFORMATION PER SERVING

Calories	176	Saturated Fat (g)	0
Protein (g)	7	Dietary Fiber (g)	6
Carbohydrate (g)	39	Cholesterol (mg)	0
Fat (g)	1	Sodium (mg)	393
Cal. from Fat (%)	4		

Diabetic Exchanges: 1.5 starch, 3 vegetable

SPLIT PEA SOUP

There's always someone who loves split pea soup.

2 cups dried split peas	1 bay leaf
5 slices turkey bacon, cut into pieces	2 cups sliced carrots
1 onion, chopped	1 potato, peeled and diced
½ cup chopped celery	Salt and pepper to taste
4 cups canned fat-free chicken broth	½ teaspoon dried thyme leaves

Soak peas in water to cover overnight. In large pot sauté turkey bacon, onion, and celery until tender. Add peas in water and remaining ingredients. Bring soup to boil, lower heat, and cook, covered for 1½ to 2 hours or until peas are very soft. Stir occasionally. If soup gets too thick, thin with additional broth or water. Remove bay leaf before serving.

Makes 6 servings

Doc's Notes:
Add a grilled cheese or ham sandwich and your meal is complete.

NUTRITIONAL INFORMATION PER SERVING

Calories	276	Saturated Fat (g)	1
Protein (g)	19	Dietary Fiber (g)	16
Carbohydrate (g)	46	Cholesterol (mg)	10
Fat (g)	3	Sodium (mg)	594
Cal. from Fat (%)	9		

Diabetic Exchanges: 2 very lean meat, 2 starch, 3 vegetable

SQUASH BISQUE

You may substitute two (10-ounce) packages frozen squash for fresh. This delicious soup will attract squash fans.

2 tablespoons olive oil
1 medium onion, chopped
1¼ pounds yellow squash, thinly sliced
1 cup diced carrots, about 2
2 large Yukon potatoes, peeled and diced

4 cups canned fat-free chicken broth
¼ teaspoon dried thyme leaves
Dash of paprika
Salt and pepper to taste

In a large pot, heat oil and sauté onion until tender, about 5 minutes. Add the squash and sauté, stirring, about 10 minutes. Add carrots, potato and chicken broth. Bring to a boil. Reduce heat and simmer about 30 to 40 minutes or until veggies are tender. Add thyme, paprika, and salt and pepper to taste.

Makes eight (1-cup) servings

Doc's Notes:
Squash is packed with nutrients and is an excellent source of Vitamin C and potassium.

NUTRITIONAL INFORMATION PER SERVING

Calories	97	Saturated Fat (g)	1
Protein (g)	4	Dietary Fiber (g)	3
Carbohydrate (g)	15	Cholesterol (mg)	0
Fat (g)	4	Sodium (mg)	317
Cal. from Fat (%)	30		

Diabetic Exchanges: 0.5 starch, 1.5 vegetable, 1 fat

MINESTRONE SOUP

A variety of veggies and white beans with Italian flair.

1 cup dried white beans
1 quart plus 1 cup water, divided
4 cloves garlic, minced
2 stalks celery, chopped
1 onion, chopped
1 (10-ounce) can chopped tomatoes and green chiles
1 (14½-ounce) can whole tomatoes, chopped, undrained
5¼ cups canned fat-free chicken broth
¼ cup red wine
1 tablespoon dried oregano leaves
1 tablespoon dried basil leaves
Salt and pepper to taste
2 bay leaves
1 red potato, peeled and diced
½ pound fresh green beans, cut diagonally into thirds
2 carrots, diced
⅓ cup dry elbow macaroni

Soak white beans for 6 hours in 1 quart water; pour beans with soaking liquid into a pot. Bring to a boil and add garlic, celery, and onions. Cook 1½ hours or until beans are tender. Add chopped tomato and green chiles, chopped tomatoes with juice, chicken broth, 1 cup water, red wine, oregano, basil, salt and pepper, and bay leaves. Bring to a boil. Add potato, green beans, carrots, and macaroni. Reduce heat to a simmer and cook 30 to 45 minutes or until vegetables are tender.

Makes 6 to 8 servings

Doc's Notes:
Excellent source of Vitamins A and C and fiber.

NUTRITIONAL INFORMATION PER SERVING

Calories	171	Saturated Fat (g)	0
Protein (g)	11	Dietary Fiber (g)	8
Carbohydrate (g)	32	Cholesterol (mg)	0
Fat (g)	1	Sodium (mg)	660
Cal. from Fat (%)	2		

Diabetic Exchanges: 0.5 very lean meat, 1.5 starch, 2 vegetable

SWEET POTATO AND APPLE SOUP

By blending sweet potatoes and apples with a touch of ginger and curry, you have an incredibly flavored soup that leaves a lasting impression. The toasty walnuts add the finishing touch to make this a perfect fall soup. Make ahead and refrigerate. If reheating, add more milk as needed to reach soup consistency.

½ cup chopped onions	½ teaspoon ground ginger
4 cups peeled and chopped sweet potatoes (yams)	½ teaspoon ground curry
	1 tablespoon honey
2 cups peeled, cored, and chopped baking apples	1 cup skim milk
	⅓ cup chopped walnuts, toasted
2 cups canned fat-free chicken broth	

In a nonstick pot coated with nonstick cooking spray, sauté the onions until tender. Add the sweet potatoes, apples, chicken broth, ginger, curry, and honey. Bring to a boil. Reduce heat, cover, and simmer until the potatoes are tender, about 25 minutes. Transfer to a food processor and purée until smooth. Return to pot; stir in the milk until blended. Sprinkle each serving with toasted walnuts.

Makes five (1-cup) servings

NUTRITIONAL INFORMATION PER SERVING

Calories	233	Saturated Fat (g)	1
Protein (g)	6	Dietary Fiber (g)	5
Carbohydrate (g)	41	Cholesterol (mg)	1
Fat (g)	6	Sodium (mg)	288
Cal. from Fat (%)	22		

Diabetic Exchanges: 2 starch, 0.5 fruit, 1 fat

WALDORF SALAD

This recipe is a healthy update on a classic. The salad is an excellent source of fiber, vitamins and minerals.

6	cups peeled and chopped apples (red and yellow)	½	cup chopped walnuts, toasted
2	stalks celery, chopped	½	cup raisins
1	cup red or green seedless grapes	1	cup nonfat plain yogurt
		¼	cup light mayonnaise
		¼	cup fresh orange juice

In a mixing bowl combine apples, celery, grapes, walnuts, and raisins. In another bowl, mix yogurt, mayonnaise, and orange juice. Toss the dressing with the salad ingredients and chill.

Makes 8 to 10 servings

Doc's Notes:

This is not only filled with fiber, but is very colorful and will surely stimulate your taste buds. For added calories, don't use fat-free products.

NUTRITIONAL INFORMATION PER SERVING

Calories	153	Saturated Fat (g)	1
Protein (g)	3	Dietary Fiber (g)	3
Carbohydrate (g)	24	Cholesterol (mg)	3
Fat (g)	6	Sodium (mg)	76
Cal. from Fat (%)	35		

Diabetic Exchanges: 1.5 fruit, 1 fat

CHICKEN SALAD

Use leftover chicken to create this
delicious salad filled with fruit and flavor.

3	cups cooked chicken breasts, cut in chunks.	⅓	cup light mayonnaise
1	cup chopped celery	1	tablespoon lemon juice
¾	pound red and green grapes	1	tablespoon soy sauce
		1	large apple, chopped
		¼	cup pecans, toasted

In a large bowl, combine chicken, celery, and grapes. In a small bowl, mix together mayonnaise, lemon juice, and soy sauce. Toss dressing with chicken mixture. Refrigerate until serving. Just before serving, mix in apples and pecans.

Makes 6 to 8 servings

Doc's Notes:

You will find this salad to be a great source of fiber. Great dish to enjoy if your bowels are a bit sluggish. Apples are a great source of fiber.

NUTRITIONAL INFORMATION PER SERVING

Calories	193	Saturated Fat (g)	1
Protein (g)	17	Dietary Fiber (g)	2
Carbohydrate (g)	14	Cholesterol (mg)	48
Fat (g)	8	Sodium (mg)	241
Cal. from Fat (%)	37		

Diabetic Exchanges: 2 very lean meat, 1 fruit, 1 fat

MANDARIN CHICKEN SALAD

This super chicken salad combined with fruit and water chestnut; and tossed with a light lemon dressing is hard to beat.

1½ pounds skinless, boneless chicken breasts, cut into chunks
1 tablespoon canola oil
4 tablespoons reduced-sodium soy sauce, divided
½ teaspoon minced garlic
¼ teaspoon ground ginger
1 cup green grapes, cut in half
1 cup chopped celery

½ cup thinly sliced green onions (scallions)
1 (11-ounce) can mandarin orange segments in water drained
1 (8-ounce) can sliced water chestnuts, drained
1 (6-ounce) container nonfat lemon yogurt
6 cups (loosely packed) washed, stemmed, torn spinach leaves

In a bowl, combine the chicken, oil, 2 tablespoons soy sauce, garlic, and ginger, coating the chicken well. In a skillet coated with nonstick cooking spray, cook the chicken mixture over medium heat, about 5 to 7 minutes, until the chicken is done. Set aside and let cool. In a bowl, combine the chicken, grapes, celery, green onions, orange segments, and water chestnuts. Mix together the yogurt and remaining 2 tablespoons soy sauce and pour over the chicken mixture. Cover and refrigerate until the mixture is well chilled, about 2 hours. Serve on the spinach leaves.

Makes 4 to 6 servings

Doc's Notes:
This is filled with fiber and Vitamin C. This is a great salad to help keep those bowels moving.

NUTRITIONAL INFORMATION PER SERVING

Calories	241	Saturated Fat (g)	1
Protein (g)	30	Dietary Fiber (g)	3
Carbohydrate (g)	21	Cholesterol (mg)	66
Fat (g)	4	Sodium (mg)	542
Cal. from Fat (%)	15		

Diabetic Exchanges: 3 very lean meat, 1 fruit, 1 vegetable

SHRIMP AND WILD RICE SALAD

Adjust the veggies in this salad to your preference and availability. For a vegetarian delight, just delete the shrimp.

1 (6-ounce) box long-grain and wild rice
1 cup cooked rice
4 cups broccoli florets
1 pound cooked and peeled medium shrimp
1 cup sliced carrots
½ pound mushrooms, sliced
1 cup thinly sliced zucchini
1 cup thinly sliced yellow squash
½ cup red bell pepper, cored and chopped
1 bunch green onions (scallions), sliced
3 large hard-boiled eggs, whites only, finely chopped
⅔ cup nonfat plain yogurt
3 tablespoons light mayonnaise
Salt and pepper to taste

Cook the wild rice according to package directions; set aside. In a large bowl, combine the wild rice, rice, broccoli, shrimp, carrots, mushrooms, zucchini, squash, red pepper, onions, and egg whites. In a small bowl, stir together the yogurt and mayonnaise. Pour the yogurt mixture over the shrimp mixture; toss lightly. Season with salt and pepper. Cover and refrigerate.

Makes 6 servings

Doc's Notes:
A cup of this salad makes a great snack any time of day. It is high in fiber and contains beta carotene, vitamins, minerals, and a cruciferous vegetable.

NUTRITIONAL INFORMATION PER SERVING

Calories	306	Saturated Fat (g)	1
Protein (g)	26	Dietary Fiber (g)	4
Carbohydrate (g)	42	Cholesterol (mg)	151
Fat (g)	4	Sodium (mg)	724
Cal. from Fat (%)	12		

Diabetic Exchanges: 3 very lean meat, 2 starch, 2 vegetable

TUNA PASTA SALAD

This simple and sensational salad takes tuna to a new level.

1 (16-ounce) package tri-colored rotini
1 bunch fresh broccoli cut into florets
2 medium tomatoes, cut into chunks
¼ cup pitted ripe olives, chopped
½ onion, cut into thin slices, rings separated
1 (12-ounce) can solid white tuna in spring water, drained
⅓ cup balsamic vinegar
¼ cup lemon juice
1 tablespoon water
2 tablespoons olive oil
2 tablespoons Dijon mustard
½ teaspoon pepper

Cook the pasta according to package directions, omitting any salt and oil. Drain and combine with the broccoli florets, tomatoes, olives, onion, and tuna. Set aside. In a small bowl, combine the vinegar, lemon juice, water, olive oil, mustard, and pepper. Beat with a fork vigorously. Pour over the pasta mixture. Toss gently. Chill 2 hours. Toss gently before serving.

Makes 8 to 10 servings

Doc's Notes:

Good source of protein and fiber as well as Vitamins A and C. Broccoli provides your cruciferous vegetable which is linked to cancer protection.

NUTRITIONAL INFORMATION PER SERVING

Calories	267	Saturated Fat (g)	1
Protein (g)	15	Dietary Fiber (g)	2
Carbohydrate (g)	40	Cholesterol (mg)	14
Fat (g)	5	Sodium (mg)	245
Cal. from Fat (%)	17		

Diabetic Exchanges: 1 very lean meat, 2 starch, 2 vegetable, 0.5 fat

BLACK AND WHITE BEAN SALAD

Here's an updated bean salad with a
Southwestern flair. Add beans of your choice.

1 (15-ounce) can white (cannellini or navy) beans, rinsed and drained
1 (15-ounce) can black beans, rinsed and drained
1 cup chopped tomato
1 cup sliced green onions (scallions)

½ cup chopped red bell pepper
½ cup picante sauce
¼ cup balsamic vinegar
½ teaspoon minced garlic
1 tablespoon olive oil
2 tablespoons chopped fresh cilantro, optional

In a large bowl, combine white beans, black beans, tomato, green onions, and red pepper. In a small bowl, whisk together picante sauce, balsamic vinegar, garlic, olive oil, and cilantro. Toss with salad and refrigerate until serving.

Makes eight (½-cup) servings

Doc's Notes:
Beans are high in protein, carbs, and fiber.

NUTRITIONAL INFORMATION PER SERVING

Calories	125	Saturated Fat (g)	0
Protein (g)	5	Dietary Fiber (g)	6
Carbohydrate (g)	20	Cholesterol (mg)	0
Fat (g)	2	Sodium (mg)	364
Cal. from Fat (%)	18		

Diabetic Exchanges: 1 starch, 1 vegetable

BLACK BEAN AND CORN SALAD

A quick and delicious salad that adds to any plate.
Serve with chicken or fish as a condiment.

1   (15-ounce) can black beans, drained and rinsed
1   (11-ounce) can golden sweet corn, drained
1   tomato, chopped
¼   cup fresh chopped cilantro

2   tablespoons chopped red onion
3   tablespoons lemon juice
2   tablespoons olive oil
Salt and pepper to taste

Combine all ingredients in bowl. Refrigerate until ready to serve.

Makes 6 servings

NUTRITIONAL INFORMATION PER SERVING

Calories	142	Saturated Fat (g)	1
Protein (g)	5	Dietary Fiber (g)	5
Carbohydrate (g)	19	Cholesterol (mg)	0
Fat (g)	6	Sodium (mg)	294
Cal. from Fat (%)	34		

Diabetic Exchanges: 0.5 very lean meat, 1.5 starch, 1 fat

BAKED BEANS

This is an easy version of an old-fashioned recipe. If desired, you can leave out the bacon for a vegetarian dish.

1 onion, chopped
1 green bell pepper, cored and chopped
3 ounces Canadian bacon, cut in ½-inch pieces, optional
2 (15-ounce) cans red kidney beans, drained
2 (19-ounce) cans white kidney beans (cannellini), drained
2 tablespoons Worcestershire sauce
½ cup light brown sugar
⅔ cup barbecue sauce
1 teaspoon dry mustard

Preheat oven to 350 degrees. In a large skillet coated with nonstick cooking spray, sauté the onion and green pepper until tender, about 4 minutes. Add the Canadian bacon. Cook for 5 more minutes. Place all the beans in a 2-quart casserole dish and add the sautéed vegetables, Worcestershire sauce, brown sugar, barbecue sauce, and mustard. Mix well. Bake, covered, for 40 minutes.

Makes 12 servings

Doc's Notes:
Beans provide a good source of protein, potassium, and iron.

NUTRITIONAL INFORMATION PER SERVING

Calories	185	Saturated Fat (g)	0
Protein (g)	8	Dietary Fiber (g)	8
Carbohydrate (g)	36	Cholesterol (mg)	0
Fat (g)	1	Sodium (mg)	484
Cal. from Fat (%)	5		

Diabetic Exchanges: 0.5 very lean meat, 1.5 starch, 1 other carb.

BASIC BROCCOLI

Broccoli with flavor. For a time saver, buy broccoli crowns.

4-6 cups broccoli florets
½ cup water

½ teaspoon chicken bouillon granules (or ½ cup chicken broth but delete water)

In microwave-safe dish, place all ingredients. Cover with plastic wrap and microwave for 6 to 8 minutes or until broccoli is tender.

Doc's Notes: *Makes 4 to 6 servings*

Broccoli is a cruciferous family veggie. The indoles found in broccoli are felt to be effective in protecting against certain forms of cancer.

NUTRITIONAL INFORMATION PER SERVING

Calories	22	Saturated Fat (g)	0
Protein (g)	2	Dietary Fiber (g)	2
Carbohydrate (g)	4	Cholesterol (mg)	0
Fat (g)	0	Sodium (mg)	159
Cal. from Fat (%)	0		

Diabetic Exchanges: 1 vegetable

BAKED CORN CASSEROLE

Use plain canned tomatoes for a less spicy version.

1 cup onion, chopped
1 tablespoon margarine
1 (10-ounce) can diced tomatoes and green chiles

1 (16-ounce) can whole-kernel yellow corn, drained
1 (15-ounce) can shoe peg white corn, drained
1 (15-ounce) can cream-style corn

In a pot, sauté onion in margarine until soft. Add tomatoes, whole-kernel corn, shoe peg corn, and creamed corn. Refrigerate for at least 8 hours or overnight. Bake at 325 degrees for 1 hour.

Doc's Notes: *Makes 6 servings*

Tomatoes provide Vitamins A and C.

NUTRITIONAL INFORMATION PER SERVING

Calories	191	Saturated Fat (g)	1
Protein (g)	5	Dietary Fiber (g)	4
Carbohydrate (g)	39	Cholesterol (mg)	0
Fat (g)	3	Sodium (mg)	700
Cal. from Fat (%)	14		

Diabetic Exchanges: 2.5 starch, 1 vegetable

TASTY BROWN RICE

Here's a little twist to jazz up your rice. Brown rice adds flavor and fiber. The veggies may be omitted for a basic brown rice recipe.

1   tablespoon olive oil
½   cup finely chopped onion
½   teaspoon minced garlic
1   (16-ounce) package assorted veggies (broccoli, carrot, and snow peas), about 8 cups
1   cup dry brown rice

½   cup diced tomato
½   bay leaf
1¾ cups canned fat-free chicken broth
½   cup water
3   tablespoons grated Parmesan cheese

Preheat oven to 350 degrees. In a large pot, heat olive oil and sauté the onion, garlic and assorted veggies over medium heat, stirring until tender. Add the rice, tomato, bay leaf, broth and water. Stir until well mixed. Cover and bring to a boil. Reduce heat and cook until rice is done, about 20 to 30 minutes. Remove bay leaf. Stir in cheese.

Makes 6 to 8 servings

NUTRITIONAL INFORMATION PER SERVING

Calories	141	Saturated Fat (g)	1
Protein (g)	5	Dietary Fiber (g)	2
Carbohydrate (g)	23	Cholesterol (mg)	2
Fat (g)	3	Sodium (mg)	199
Cal. from Fat (%)	20		

Diabetic Exchanges: 1 starch, 0.5 fat, 1 vegetable

WILD RICE AND BARLEY PILAF

A nice alternative to replace a rice dish.

1 (6-ounce) package long grain and wild rice
½ cup pearl barley

3 cups canned fat-free chicken broth
1 tablespoon margarine
⅓ cup sliced almonds, toasted

Preheat oven to 325 degrees. In saucepan, combine rice, seasoning packet, barley, chicken broth, and margarine. Bring to a boil. Reduce heat, cover, and simmer for 10 minutes. Spoon into a 1½-quart casserole dish. Bake, covered, for 1 hour or until rice and barley are tender and liquid is absorbed. Fluff rice mixture with a fork; stir in almonds.

Makes 6 to 8 servings

Doc's Notes:
Rice, salad and a grilled chicken breast is quick, simple, and filling. The wild rice and barley provide a good source of fiber.

NUTRITIONAL INFORMATION PER SERVING

Calories	162	Saturated Fat (g)	0
Protein (g)	5	Dietary Fiber (g)	3
Carbohydrate (g)	28	Cholesterol (mg)	0
Fat (g)	4	Sodium (mg)	566
Cal. from Fat (%)	20		

Diabetic Exchanges: 2 starch, 0.5 fat

VEGGIE ANGEL HAIR

You can substitute your favorite veggies to create a version that suits your taste buds. This is a great veggie dish or main dish on a meatless night.

1 (16-ounce) package angel hair pasta
2 tablespoons olive oil
1 cup chopped onion
1 tablespoon minced garlic
2 medium zucchini, cut into 2x½-inch pieces
1 cup frozen corn
¼ cup water
1 teaspoon dried dill weed
¼ cup grated Parmesan cheese
¼ cup chopped pecans, toasted, optional

Cook the pasta according to package directions until done. Drain and set aside. In a large skillet heat the olive oil, sauté the onion and garlic until tender. Add the zucchini, corn and ¼ cup water to the skillet, cover and cook the vegetables over medium heat about 5 minutes, or until just tender. Add the pasta and toss with dill and Parmesan cheese, stirring until heated through. Mix in pecans, if desired.

Makes 4 main dish servings

Makes 6 to 8 side servings

NUTRITIONAL INFORMATION PER MAIN DISH SERVING

Calories 469
Protein (g) 16
Carbohydrate (g) 79
Fat (g) 11
Cal. from Fat (%) 20
Saturated Fat (g) 2
Dietary Fiber (g) 5
Cholesterol (mg) 5
Sodium (mg) 129

Diabetic Exchanges: 5 starch, 1 vegetable, 1 fat

YAM VEGGIE WRAPS

A quick and wonderful flavor combo that makes a nutritious wrap to remember. Shred sweet potatoes on grater or in a food processor.

1	sweet potato (yam), peeled and shredded (about 1 cup)	¼	cup sunflower seeds
½	cup chopped red onion	2	tablespoons light Italian or Caesar dressing
1	cup black beans, rinsed and drained	1	teaspoon honey
2	green onions (scallions), sliced	6	flour tortillas, warmed to soften

In a skillet coated with nonstick cooking spray, sauté shredded yams over medium high heat for about 5 minutes or until crisp tender. Transfer to a bowl. In same skillet coated with nonstick cooking spray, sauté red onion for about 5 minutes until tender. Add sautéed onion, black beans, green onions, and sunflower seeds to shredded yams, mixing well. In a small bowl, mix together dressing and honey and toss with yam mixture to coat. Fill tortillas with mixture and wrap.

Makes 6 wraps

Doc's Notes:
Sweet Potatoes are one of the most nutritious vegetables.

NUTRITIONAL INFORMATION PER SERVING

Calories	200	Saturated Fat (g)	1
Protein (g)	7	Dietary Fiber (g)	5
Carbohydrate (g)	32	Cholesterol (mg)	0
Fat (g)	5	Sodium (mg)	231
Cal. from Fat (%)	23		

Diabetic Exchanges: 2 starch, 0.5 fat

VEGETABLE LASAGNA

Lasagna makes a great meal, freezes well, and can be made ahead.

1   onion, chopped
3   cloves garlic, minced
1   green bell pepper, cored and chopped
1   (6-ounce) can tomato paste
1   (10-ounce) can diced tomatoes and green chiles
1   (10-ounce) can stewed tomatoes
1   (11½-ounce) can tomato juice
1   teaspoon dried basil leaves
1   teaspoon dried oregano leaves

1   teaspoon dried thyme leaves
1½ tablespoons red wine vinegar
1   bay leaf
½   pound fresh mushrooms, sliced
½   cup shredded carrot
1   bunch broccoli flowerets
½   pound lasagna noodles
1½ cups shredded part-skim mozzarella cheese

Preheat oven to 350 degrees. Coat a large skillet with nonstick cooking spray and add onion, garlic and green pepper. Sauté until tender. Add tomato paste, diced tomatoes and green chiles, stewed tomatoes, and tomato juice. Bring to a boil. Add remaining ingredients except lasagna noodles and cheese. Reduce heat and simmer at least 30 minutes or until vegetables are tender and sauce has slightly thickened. Discard bay leaf. Cook lasagna noodles according to directions on package omitting salt and oil; drain. Spoon some vegetable sauce over the bottom of a 13x9x2-inch baking dish. Layer one-third each of lasagna noodles, Cheese Mixture (recipe follows), remaining vegetable sauce, and mozzarella cheese. Repeat layers twice. Bake, covered, for 30 minutes. Let stand 10 minutes before cutting.

Cheese Mixture
2   cups low fat cottage cheese
1   large egg white
2   tablespoons chopped parsley
¼   cup grated Parmesan cheese

Combine all ingredients in a food processor, blending well.

Makes 12 servings

Doc's Notes:
Filled with Vitamins A, C, and minerals. Broccoli provides the cruciferous vegetable.

(see Nutritional Information on next page)

NUTRITIONAL INFORMATION PER SERVING

Calories	192	Saturated Fat (g)	2
Protein (g)	14	Dietary Fiber (g)	3
Carbohydrate (g)	26	Cholesterol (mg)	12
Fat (g)	4	Sodium (mg)	558
Cal. from Fat (%)	17		

Diabetic Exchanges: 1.5 lean meat, 1 starch, 2 vegetable

RED BEANS AND RICE

An excellent choice for a true Louisiana dish.

1 **pound dried red kidney beans**
1 **pound turkey sausage, thinly sliced**
1 **large onion, chopped**
½ **cup chopped celery**
1 **cup chopped green onion (scallions)**
½ **cup chopped parsley**
2 **cloves garlic, minced**
8 **cups water**
2 **bay leaves**
1 **tablespoon Worcestershire sauce**
Dash of hot pepper sauce
Salt and pepper to taste

In a large bowl, soak red beans in hot water to cover for at least 1 hour. Drain and set aside. In a large pot, cook turkey sausage until done. Add the onion, celery, green onion, parsley, and garlic and sauté until tender. Add beans, 8 cups water, and remaining ingredients. Bring to a boil. Reduce heat, cover, and cook for 30 minutes. Remove cover and cook on low heat for 1½ hours or until beans are tender. Serve over cooked rice.

Makes 6 to 8 servings

Doc's Notes:

This is an excellent source of fiber. Try serving over brown rice for even more fiber.

NUTRITIONAL INFORMATION PER SERVING

Calories	284	Saturated Fat (g)	2
Protein (g)	22	Dietary Fiber (g)	14
Carbohydrate (g)	35	Cholesterol (mg)	47
Fat (g)	7	Sodium (mg)	382
Cal. from Fat (%)	20		

Diabetic Exchanges: 2 lean meat, 2 starch, 1 vegetable

SOUTHWESTERN PASTA

Vegetarians as well as pasta lovers will put this southwestern recipe high on their lists. Place tomatoes in food processor to purée or purchase diced tomatoes.

1 (28-ounce) can no-salt added whole tomatoes, puréed, with their juice
1 onion, chopped
1½ teaspoons chili powder
½ teaspoon cumin
1 teaspoon dried oregano leaves
½ teaspoon minced garlic
½ teaspoon sugar
¼ teaspoon ground cinnamon
¼ teaspoon red pepper flakes, optional
Salt and pepper to taste
1 (16-ounce) package rotini
1 (16-ounce) can black beans, drained and rinsed
1 (10-ounce) package frozen corn
1 (4½-ounce) can chopped green chiles, drained
1 cup shredded reduced-fat Cheddar cheese, optional

Heat a large pot coated with nonstick cooking spray to medium heat, and add the tomato purée, onion, chili powder, cumin, oregano, garlic, sugar, cinnamon, red pepper flakes, and salt and pepper. Bring to a boil, reduce heat, and simmer, covered, to blend the flavors, 20 to 25 minutes. Meanwhile, cook the pasta according to package directions, omitting any oil and salt. Drain well. Stir the black beans, corn, and green chiles into the sauce. Cook until the corn is crisp-tender, about 5 minutes. Remove from the heat. To serve, toss the black bean mixture with the pasta. If desired, serve with reduced-fat Cheddar cheese.

Makes 6 to 8 servings

NUTRITIONAL INFORMATION PER SERVING

Calories	323	Saturated Fat (g)	0
Protein (g)	13	Dietary Fiber (g)	7
Carbohydrate (g)	65	Cholesterol (mg)	0
Fat (g)	2	Sodium (mg)	240
Cal. from Fat (%)	5		

Diabetic Exchanges: 4 starch, 1 vegetable

MEAT LOAF

Sometimes a comfort food such as meat loaf hits the spot.
The chili sauce topping adds that finishing touch.
Raid a salad bar for shredded carrots.
Cut recipe in half and place in smaller
loaf pan for smaller meat loaf.

1½ pounds ground sirloin
2 large egg whites
1 carrot, shredded (about ½ cup)
1 teaspoon dried oregano leaves
1 teaspoon dried basil leaves
Salt and pepper to taste
½ cup old-fashioned oatmeal
1 cup tomato juice
⅓ cup chili sauce

Preheat oven to 350 degrees. Mix together ground sirloin, egg whites, carrot, oregano, basil, and salt and pepper. In a small bowl, mix together oatmeal and tomato juice, let sit for 5 minutes and combine with meat mixture. Transfer to a 9x5x3-inch loaf pan and bake for 40 minutes. Remove from oven and cover top with chili sauce. Return to oven for 20 minutes longer. Drain any excess grease.

Makes 8 servings

NUTRITIONAL INFORMATION PER SERVING

Calories	188	Saturated Fat (g)	3
Protein (g)	20	Dietary Fiber (g)	1
Carbohydrate (g)	9	Cholesterol (mg)	31
Fat (g)	8	Sodium (mg)	340
Cal. from Fat (%)	39		

Diabetic Exchanges: 2.5 lean meat, 0.5 starch

ALL NATURAL LAXATIVE

This is not a flavor savor but it works.

1¼ cups unprocessed bran
1 cup prune juice

1 tablespoon molasses or honey
1 cup applesauce

Mix and store in a covered container in the refrigerator for up to 7 days. Stir before taking. Take 2 tablespoons every night as needed.

Makes 18 (2 tablespoon) servings

Doc's Notes:
If 2 tablespoons caused diarrhea, decrease to 1 tablespoon. If you find that 2 tablespoons is not enough, you can increase to 3 or 4 tablespoons. If this combination is not working, you can also take a laxative. The prune juice comes in 6 packs of (5½-ounce) cans. The high fiber content acts by drawing water into the colon, softening your stool and aiding in bowel movements. Always drink fluids to increase the effectiveness of the fiber.

NUTRITIONAL INFORMATION PER SERVING

Calories	28	Saturated Fat (g)	0
Protein (g)	1	Dietary Fiber (g)	2
Carbohydrate (g)	7	Cholesterol (mg)	0
Fat (g)	0	Sodium (mg)	1
Cal. from Fat (%)	0		

Diabetic Exchanges: 0.5 fruit

ZUCCHINI OATMEAL-RAISIN MUFFINS

These are a grainy not so sweet muffin. Their versatility makes them great for breakfast, a snack, or with a bowl of soup or salad.

1½ cups buttermilk	1 cup whole wheat flour
1 cup old-fashioned oatmeal	1 teaspoon baking powder
2 tablespoons margarine, softened	1 teaspoon baking soda
	1 teaspoon ground cinnamon
½ cup light brown sugar	1 cup shredded zucchini
1 large egg, lightly beaten	½ cup golden raisins
½ cup all-purpose flour	

Preheat oven to 400 degrees. In a medium bowl, stir together the buttermilk and oatmeal; set aside for 15 minutes. In another mixing bowl, cream together the margarine and brown sugar. Beat in the egg. In another bowl, combine the flours, baking powder, baking soda, and cinnamon. Add the oatmeal mixture alternately with the dry ingredients to the creamed mixture and stir to combine. Stir in the zucchini and raisins. Divide the batter among the muffin tin cups and bake for 20 to 25 minutes, or until a toothpick inserted in the center of a muffin comes out clean.

Makes 12 muffins

Doc's Notes:

I recommend a high fiber muffin such as this one daily. If you are taking any type narcotic pain medicine, you need the extra fiber daily. The narcotic medicines slow the normal contractile activity of the bowels, leading to constipation. By adding fiber and fluids, you promote bowel activity.

NUTRITIONAL INFORMATION PER SERVING

Calories	170	Saturated Fat (g)	1
Protein (g)	5	Dietary Fiber (g)	3
Carbohydrate (g)	32	Cholesterol (mg)	19
Fat (g)	3	Sodium (mg)	211
Cal. from Fat (%)	17		

Diabetic Exchanges: 1 starch, 0.5 fruit, 0.5 other carb., 0.5 fat

SWEET POTATO, APPLE, AND WALNUT MUFFINS

The tartness of apples and raisins combined with the sweetness of yams and flavorful walnuts create a moist muffin that will quickly become one of your favorites.

1¾ cups all-purpose flour
1½ teaspoons baking powder
1   teaspoon ground cinnamon
3   tablespoons canola oil
¾   cup light brown sugar
1   large egg
1   large egg white

1   (15-ounce) can sweet potatoes (yams), drained and mashed
½   cup skim milk
1¾ cups chopped and peeled baking apples
⅓   cup chopped walnuts
⅓   cup golden raisins

Preheat oven to 400 degrees. Coat 18 muffin tin cups with nonstick cooking spray or line with paper liners. In a bowl, mix together flour, baking powder, and cinnamon; set aside. In another bowl, mix together the oil, brown sugar, egg, egg white, mashed sweet potatoes, and milk until well mixed. Make a well in the center of the dry ingredients and add potato mixture, stirring until moistened. Do not overmix. Fold in the apples, walnuts, and raisins. Spoon batter into prepared muffin tins, filling about three-fourths full. Bake for 20 to 25 minutes or until done.

Makes 18 muffins

Doc's Notes:
Apples provide fiber, Vitamin C, potassium and boron. Apples are fibrous, juicy, and non-sticky, making them a good tooth cleaner and gum stimulator.

NUTRITIONAL INFORMATION PER SERVING

Calories 150
Protein (g) 3
Carbohydrate (g) 26
Fat (g) 4
Cal. from Fat (%) 25
Saturated Fat (g) 0
Dietary Fiber (g) 1
Cholesterol (mg) 12
Sodium (mg) 62

Diabetic Exchanges: 1 starch, 0.5 fruit, 0.5 other carb., 0.5 fat

HONEY BRAN PRUNE MUFFINS

An intensive intake of fiber into a tasty muffin.

2   cups wheat bran
2   cups all-purpose flour
⅛   teaspoon salt
1   teaspoon baking soda
½   cup light brown sugar
3   large eggs

1   cup prune juice
½   cup canola oil or
    applesauce
½   cup honey
1   cup raisins

Preheat oven to 400 degrees. In a bowl, combine bran, flour, salt, baking soda, and brown sugar. Add eggs, prune juice, oil or applesauce, and honey, mixing well. Stir in raisins. Pour batter into paper lined muffin tins. Bake for 20 minutes.

Makes 18 muffins

Doc's Notes:
These can be used as a bread with any meal. Excellent breakfast food.

NUTRITIONAL INFORMATION PER SERVING

Calories	219	Saturated Fat (g)	1
Protein (g)	4	Dietary Fiber (g)	4
Carbohydrate (g)	38	Cholesterol (mg)	35
Fat (g)	7	Sodium (mg)	103
Cal. from Fat (%)	28		

Diabetic Exchanges: 1 starch, 1 other carb., 0.5 fruit, 1 fat

BANANA BRAN MUFFINS

Even my kids loved these muffins. Wheat bran is found in the natural health food section in the grocery or health food store.

1 cup all-purpose flour	¼ cup canola oil
1 cup wheat bran	½ cup light brown sugar
1 teaspoon baking soda	1 large egg
½ teaspoon ground cinnamon	½ cup chopped walnuts,
1 cup mashed banana	optional

Preheat oven to 375 degrees. In a bowl, mix together the flour, wheat bran, baking soda, and cinnamon; set aside. In a mixing bowl, beat together banana and oil. Add the brown sugar and egg, mixing well. Add the dry ingredients, stirring just until blended. Stir in walnuts. Spoon into paper lined muffin tins. Bake 15 minutes.

Makes 12 muffins

NUTRITIONAL INFORMATION PER SERVING

Calories 147	Saturated Fat (g) 1
Protein (g) 3	Dietary Fiber (g) 3
Carbohydrate (g) 25	Cholesterol (mg) 18
Fat (g) 5	Sodium (mg) 114
Cal. from Fat (%).................. 31	

Diabetic Exchanges: 1 starch, 0.5 fruit, 1 fat

STRAWBERRY BREAD

Another great bread made with one of my favorite fruits. Strawberries are available year round.

2 cups all-purpose flour
¾ cup sugar
1½ teaspoons baking powder
½ teaspoon baking soda
1 large egg
1 large egg white

⅓ cup margarine, melted
⅓ cup cranberry juice cocktail or orange juice
2 teaspoons grated lemon rind
1½ cups coarsely chopped strawberries

Preheat oven to 350 degrees. Coat a 9x5x3-inch loaf pan with non-stick cooking spray. In a large bowl, mix flour, sugar, baking powder, and baking soda. Beat egg and egg white slightly in a small bowl; stir in margarine, juice and lemon rind. Add to flour mixture, stirring until well combined. Stir in berries. Pour batter into prepared pan. Bake for 50 to 60 minutes or until a toothpick inserted in bread comes out clean; cover loosely with foil if it browns too fast. Remove from pan to a wire rack to cool completely.

Makes 16 slices

Doc's Notes:
Use half whole wheat flour and half all-purpose for added fiber.

NUTRITIONAL INFORMATION PER SERVING

Calories	141	Saturated Fat (g)	1
Protein (g)	2	Dietary Fiber (g)	1
Carbohydrate (g)	23	Cholesterol (mg)	13
Fat (g)	4	Sodium (mg)	137
Cal. from Fat (%)	27		

Diabetic Exchanges: 1 starch, 0.5 other carb., 0.5 fat

LEMON BERRY BREAD

*Lemon and berries join together to make this
bread a real winner. When blueberries are not in
season, leave them out for a delicious lemon bread.*

⅓	cup canola oil	1	teaspoon baking powder
⅔	cup sugar	½	cup skim milk
2	tablespoons lemon extract	1	cup fresh blueberries
4	large egg whites	2	tablespoons grated lemon
1½	cups all-purpose flour		rind

Preheat oven to 350 degrees. In a large bowl, mix oil, sugar, lemon
extract, and egg whites. In another bowl, combine flour with baking
powder. Add flour mixture to sugar mixture alternately with milk, stirring
just until blended. Fold in blueberries and lemon rind. Pour batter into
a 9x5x3-inch loaf pan coated with nonstick cooking spray and dusted
with flour. Bake for 40 to 50 minutes or until a wooden toothpick
inserted in center comes out clean. Immediately poke holes at 1-inch
intervals into the top of the bread and pour Lemon Glaze (recipe
follows) over.

Lemon Glaze

½	cup sugar	½	cup lemon juice

In a small saucepan, combine sugar and lemon juice, heating until
sugar is dissolved.

Makes 16 servings

NUTRITIONAL INFORMATION PER SERVING

Calories	158	Saturated Fat (g)	0
Protein (g)	3	Dietary Fiber (g)	1
Carbohydrate (g)	26	Cholesterol (mg)	0
Fat (g)	5	Sodium (mg)	49
Cal. from Fat (%)	26		

Diabetic Exchanges: 1 starch, 1 other carb., 1 fat

CRANBERRY YAM BREAD

The sweetness of the yams combined with the tartness of cranberries make this bread one of my very personal favorites.

2 large eggs, slightly beaten	1 teaspoon vanilla extract
1⅓ cups sugar	1½ cups all-purpose flour
⅓ cup canola oil	1 teaspoon ground cinnamon
1 cup mashed sweet potatoes (yams), canned or cooked fresh	¼ teaspoon ground allspice
	1 teaspoon baking soda
	1 cup chopped cranberries

Preheat oven to 350 degrees. Coat a 9x5x3-inch loaf pan with non-stick cooking spray and dust with flour. In a large bowl, combine eggs, sugar, oil, yams and vanilla. In a separate bowl, combine flour, cinnamon, allspice, and baking soda. Make a well in the center. Pour yam mixture into well. Mix just until moistened. Stir in cranberries. Spoon batter into prepared loaf pan. Bake for 1 hour or until a toothpick in center comes out clean.

Makes 12 slices

Doc's Notes:
A good source of fiber and protein as well as Vitamin C and potassium.

NUTRITIONAL INFORMATION PER SERVING

Calories	237	Saturated Fat (g)	1
Protein (g)	3	Dietary Fiber (g)	1
Carbohydrate (g)	41	Cholesterol (mg)	35
Fat (g)	7	Sodium (mg)	132
Cal. from Fat (%)	27		

Diabetic Exchanges: 1 starch, 1.5 other carb., 1 fat

OATMEAL CHOCOLATE CAKE

This moist cake with chocolate laced through makes a great snack. For a chocolate spice cake version, leave out the chocolate chips and add 1 teaspoon cinnamon and ½ teaspoon allspice.

1½ cups boiling water	2 large egg whites
1 cup old-fashioned oatmeal	1 teaspoon vanilla extract
1 cup light brown sugar	1½ cups all-purpose flour
½ cupsugar	1 teaspoon baking soda
¼ cup canola oil	1 tablespoon cocoa
⅓ cup buttermilk	½ cup semisweet chocolate
1 large egg	chips

Preheat oven to 350 degrees. Coat a 13x9x2-inch baking pan with nonstick cooking spray. Pour the boiling water over the oatmeal in a bowl; let stand for 10 minutes. Add the brown sugar, sugar, oil, and buttermilk, stirring well. Add the egg, egg whites, and vanilla, mixing well. In another bowl, combine the flour, baking soda, and cocoa. Add the dry ingredients to the sugar mixture, mixing well. Stir in the chocolate chips. Pour batter into pan and bake for about 30 minutes. Let cool in pan.

Makes 24 squares

NUTRITIONAL INFORMATION PER SERVING

Calories	135	Saturated Fat (g)	1
Protein (g)	2	Dietary Fiber (g)	1
Carbohydrate (g)	24	Cholesterol (mg)	9
Fat (g)	4	Sodium (mg)	68
Cal. from Fat (%)	25		

Diabetic Exchanges: 0.5 starch, 1 other carb., 0.5 fat

PEACH CRUMBLE

Serve hot with frozen fat-free vanilla yogurt for a real treat.
This recipe works great with the fruit of your choice.

⅔ cup light brown sugar
¾ cup old-fashioned oatmeal
½ cup natural wheat and
   barley cereal
1¼ cups all-purpose flour,
   divided

1 teaspoon ground cinnamon
⅓ cup canola oil
2 (16-ounce) packages frozen
   peaches
⅔ cup confectioners' sugar
1 teaspoon vanilla extract

Preheat oven to 350 degrees. In a bowl, mix together the brown sugar, oatmeal, cereal, 1 cup flour, and cinnamon. Stir in the oil, mixing until crumbly. In another bowl, toss peaches with confectioners' sugar, vanilla, and remaining ¼ cup flour. Transfer fruit into a 2-quart baking dish and cover with oatmeal topping. Bake until bubbly, about 35 to 40 minutes.

Makes 8 to 12 servings

Doc's Notes:
The oatmeal and cereal along with the fruit pack this recipe with fiber.

NUTRITIONAL INFORMATION PER SERVING

Calories 241
Protein (g) 3
Carbohydrate (g) 42
Fat (g) 7
Cal. from Fat (%) 26
Saturated Fat (g) 1
Dietary Fiber (g) 3
Cholesterol (mg) 0
Sodium (mg) 32

Diabetic Exchanges: 1.5 starch, 0.5 fruit, 1 other carb., 1 fat

TROPICAL PIZZA

Have fun with this pizza by adding your favorite fruit and creating it in the pattern of your choice. With fresh fruit in season, this picture perfect dessert is even more nutritious.

1   (18-ounce) roll refrigerated ready to slice sugar cookie dough
⅓ cup sugar
1   (8-ounce) package fat-free cream cheese
1   teaspoon coconut extract
1½ teaspoons grated orange rind
1   cup frozen fat-free whipped topping, thawed

1   (26-ounce) jar mango slices, drained
1   (16-ounce) can pineapple slices, drained
1   (11-ounce) can mandarin orange slices, drained
¼ cup apricot preserves
1   tablespoon orange liqueur, optional
2   tablespoons coconut, toasted, optional

Preheat oven to 350 degrees. Press the cookie dough into a 12 to 14-inch pizza pan coated with nonstick cooking spray. Bake for 12 minutes and cool completely. In a mixing bowl, blend together sugar, cream cheese, and coconut extract until well mixed. Stir in the orange rind and whipped topping, mixing until smooth. Spread the cream cheese mixture on top of the cooled crust. Arrange the mango slices around the edge of the iced pizza. Next, arrange a row of the pineapple slices around the inside of the mango slices. Arrange the mandarin orange slices to fill the center of the pizza. In a small saucepan or in the microwave, heat the apricot preserves and orange liqueur just until melted. Spoon the glaze over the fruit. Sprinkle with the toasted coconut if desired. Refrigerate until serving.

Makes 12 servings

Doc's Notes:
One slice per day will aid in your constipation problem plus provide Vitamin C. Vitamins C and E, along with beta carotene are antioxidant vitamins. The antioxidants seem to neutralize a class of atomic particles known as "free radicals." The free radicals combine with other compounds, creating a chain reaction and, over the course of time, will damage cell walls and structure within the cells.

NUTRITIONAL INFORMATION PER SERVING

Calories 277	Saturated Fat (g) 2
Protein (g) 5	Dietary Fiber (g) 1
Carbohydrate (g) 51	Cholesterol (mg) 5
Fat (g) 6	Sodium (mg) 249
Cal. from Fat (%) 20	

Diabetic Exchanges: 1 starch, 1 fruit, 1.5 other carb., 1 fat

SORE MOUTH

⬧ *I have no appetite. Is there anything to help me?*
⬧ *Should I eat hot or cold foods?*
⬧ *Should I eat raw or cooked foods?*

Your mouth normally will get sore 7 to 10 days following certain chemo-therapy treatments. Remember to do your mouth care: 1 teaspoon baking soda, 1 teaspoon salt in a quart of tap water. Rinse and spit after each meal. Make a fresh solution each morning and discard at the end of the day. Try eating soft or puréed foods. Use a straw for all liquids or puréed foods. This is a good time to use plastic utensils to avoid the metallic taste. Eating foods at room temperature or cool are easier to handle when your mouth is sore. Raw foods tend to irritate your mouth and should be avoided. If you are still losing ground, talk to your physicians about the following appetite stimulants:

1—Liquid Megace – 800 mg/day x 30 days then decrease to 400 mg/day.

2—Megace 40 mg twice per day and Marinol 2.5 mg by mouth twice per day.

Remember, if you find one food that you can tolerate do not hesitate to eat it repeatedly. The mouth soreness is usually associated with a low white blood cell count. As soon as your counts rise, the soreness will resolve. Cephacol, Xylocaine, and pain medicines are sometimes needed to ease the mouth pain. I often have patients take a pain pill 30 minutes prior to meals to allow them to eat. If you have obvious sores on your lips, a small amount of Vitamin E can sometimes help. Puncture a 500 unit Vitamin E capsule and squeeze the contents on the ulcer 3 times per day.

Points to Remember

♦ Try sucking on ice chips. Popsicles or frozen juices (no orange) are soothing

♦ Use a straw for liquids.

♦ Try chewing sugar-free gum or suck on sugar-free candies.

♦ Cut food into small pieces.

♦ Eat food that is cold or at room temperature. Don't exclude hot soups; just allow it to cool to room temperature.

♦ Softer and easy to swallow foods might include soups, pastas, dairy dishes and breakfast-style recipes.

♦ Dunk drier foods in a soup or beverage before eating.

♦ Practice good oral hygiene.

♦ Drink your meals with nutritious liquids.

♦ Avoid mouth irritants such as citrus fruits and juices, and spicy, salty, or rough foods.

♦ Use oral anesthetics such as ulcerease. Ask your doctor for a "stomatitis (sore mouth) cocktail."
Xylocaine – equal parts
Maalox – equal parts
Benadryl – equal parts
Swish and swallow one teaspoonful every four hours as needed for pain.

Some Soft Foods to Include:

♦ Applesauce, bananas, watermelon, and other soft fruits.

♦ Cottage cheese.

♦ Puddings, flavored gelatin.

♦ Mashed potatoes, macaroni and cheese, or mashed sweet potatoes.

♦ Milk shakes, or smoothies.

♦ Scrambled eggs.

♦ Cooked cereals such as oatmeal or cream of wheat.

♦ Mashed veggies.

MENUS
Foods to eat when sore mouth is occurring

Breakfast
Baked French Toast (p. 26)
Banana

Egg Soufflé (p. 29)
Quick Cheese Grits (p. 58)

Applesauce Oatmeal (p. 138)

Ham and Cheese Grits Quiche (p. 145)
Soft fruits such as watermelon, papaya

Lunch
Asparagus and Potato Soup (p. 33)
Grilled Cheese Sandwich
Applesauce

Avocado Soup (p. 140)
Cheese Quesadillas (p. 166)
Mocha Meringue Mounds (p. 172)

Dinner
Quick Shrimp Sauté (p. 146)
Creamed Double Potatoes (p. 144)
Cream Cheese Bread Pudding (p. 148)

Veggie Plate
Carrot Soufflé (p. 143)
Cheesy Macaroni (p. 41)
Lemon Angel Food Cake (p. 53)

Bread Pudding Florentine (p. 28)
Quick Cheese Grits (p. 58)
Mock Chocolate Éclair (p. 54)

Snacks
Strawberry Weight Gain Shake (p. 149)
Spinach Dip (p. 157)
German Chocolate Angel Pie (p. 147)
Sweet Potato Shake (p. 140)
Cantaloupe Banana Smoothie (p. 139)
Awesome Milk Shake (p. 150)

MELON SOUP

A cool, refreshing soup or can be served in a glass for a great drink.

3 cups cubed cantaloupe
1 tablespoon lime juice
1 teaspoon sugar

1 cup nonfat plain yogurt
1 teaspoon vanilla extract

Mix together all ingredients in a food processor; process until smooth.

Makes 2 servings

Doc's Notes:
Sip through a straw until it is all gone. Great source of potassium.

NUTRITIONAL INFORMATION PER SERVING

Calories	169	Saturated Fat (g)	0
Protein (g)	9	Dietary Fiber (g)	2
Carbohydrate (g)	33	Cholesterol (mg)	2
Fat (g)	1	Sodium (mg)	116
Cal. from Fat (%)	5		

Diabetic Exchanges: 1.5 fruit, 1 skim milk

SIMPLE VICHYSSOISE

The longer it sits the better it gets!

3½ cups canned fat-free
    chicken broth
2 (10½-ounce) cans cream of
    potato soup

2 cups nonfat plain yogurt
⅓ cup chopped green onions
    (scallions), optional

In a bowl, combine broth, soup, and yogurt, mixing well. Refrigerate for several hours. Sprinkle with green onions when serving.

Makes 8 servings

NUTRITIONAL INFORMATION PER SERVING

Calories	86	Saturated Fat (g)	1
Protein (g)	6	Dietary Fiber (g)	0
Carbohydrate (g)	12	Cholesterol (mg)	5
Fat (g)	2	Sodium (mg)	926
Cal. from Fat (%)	16		

Diabetic Exchanges: 0.5 starch, 0.5 skim milk

WEIGHT GAIN PANCAKES

Top with fresh fruit or sliced bananas for added nutrition. Whole milk can be used instead of the supplement, if desired.

½ cup pancake and waffle mix
½ cup vanilla nutritional energy drink supplement
1 large egg
1 tablespoon canola oil

Preheat griddle to 400 degrees or until drops of water sizzle then evaporate on griddle. Combine all ingredients and mix with a wire whip or fork until fairly smooth. Do not overmix as this will cause thin, tough pancakes. Let batter stand 1 to 2 minutes. Pour a scant ¼ cup of batter for each pancake onto a lightly greased griddle. Turn pancakes when edges look cooked and tops are covered with bubbles. Turn only once.

Makes 6 to 7 pancakes

NUTRITIONAL INFORMATION PER SERVING

Calories 80	Saturated Fat (g) 1
Protein (g) 3	Dietary Fiber (g) 0
Carbohydrate (g) 10	Cholesterol (mg) 32
Fat (g) 3	Sodium (mg) 131
Cal. from Fat (%) 39	

Diabetic Exchanges: 0.5 starch, 0.5 fat

APPLESAUCE OATMEAL

Great way to start off your day as this recipe takes oatmeal to a new level. Instead of applesauce, try stirring in a mashed banana for banana oatmeal and, if your mouth isn't sore, add some raisins.

1 **cup skim milk**
¾ **cup old fashioned oatmeal**
½ **cup unsweetened applesauce**

1 **tablespoon light brown sugar**
⅛ **teaspoon ground cinnamon**

In a small saucepan, bring milk to a boil. Add the oatmeal and reduce heat. Cook for about 5 minutes or until thickened, stirring occasionally. Add the applesauce, brown sugar, and cinnamon, stirring until well mixed. Serve immediately.

Makes two (¾-cup) servings

NUTRITIONAL INFORMATION PER SERVING

Calories	212	Saturated Fat (g)	1
Protein (g)	9	Dietary Fiber (g)	4
Carbohydrate (g)	40	Cholesterol (mg)	2
Fat (g)	2	Sodium (mg)	68
Cal. from Fat (%)	9		

Diabetic Exchanges: 1.5 starch, 0.5 fruit, 0.5 skim milk, 0.5 other carb.

WATERMELON SLUSH

Great source of potassium and Vitamin C.

1   cup of ice   2   tablespoons honey
3   cups watermelon chunks

Blend all ingredients in a blender or food processor.

Makes 2 servings

Doc's Notes:

For cancer patients, watermelon seems to be the most tolerated fruit. It's light, cool, refreshing and goes down easy.

NUTRITIONAL INFORMATION PER SERVING

Calories 137	Saturated Fat (g) 0
Protein (g) 2	Dietary Fiber (g) 1
Carbohydrate (g) 34	Cholesterol (mg) 0
Fat (g) 1	Sodium (mg) 5
Cal. from Fat (%) 6	

Diabetic Exchanges: 1 fruit, 1 other carb.

CANTALOUPE BANANA SMOOTHIE

Fruits team up for a nutritious smoothie — potassium plus!

1   teaspoon vanilla extract   1   tablespoon honey
1   banana   1   cup reduced-fat vanilla ice
1   cup cubed cantaloupe   cream

Blend all ingredients in a blender or food processor until smooth.

Makes 2 servings

Doc's Notes:

For extra calories and nutrition, substitute vanilla nutritional drink supplement for ice cream.

NUTRITIONAL INFORMATION PER SERVING

Calories 231	Saturated Fat (g) 1
Protein (g) 4	Dietary Fiber (g) 3
Carbohydrate (g) 49	Cholesterol (mg) 5
Fat (g) 3	Sodium (mg) 53
Cal. from Fat (%) 9	

Diabetic Exchanges: 1.5 fruit, 2 other carb., 0.5 fat

SWEET POTATO SHAKE

Packed full of nutrition. Serve cold!

½ cup mashed cooked sweet potatoes (yams)
1 (12-ounce) can apricot nectar, chilled
2 tablespoons honey
½ teaspoon vanilla extract

Using a food processor, blend all ingredients until smooth. Refrigerate.

Makes 2 servings

Doc's Notes:
Rich in beta carotene and Vitamins C and B.

NUTRITIONAL INFORMATION PER SERVING

Calories	255	Saturated Fat (g)	0
Protein (g)	2	Dietary Fiber (g)	3
Carbohydrate (g)	64	Cholesterol (mg)	0
Fat (g)	0	Sodium (mg)	17
Cal. from Fat (%)	0		

Diabetic Exchanges: 1.5 starch, 1.5 fruit, 1 other carb.

AVOCADO SOUP

Avocados are a great source of monounsaturated fats.

2 large avocados, peeled and pit removed
1 teaspoon minced garlic
2 cups canned fat-free chicken broth
1 (8-ounce) bottle clam juice
½ cup nonfat plain yogurt

Using a food processor, blend all ingredients until smooth. Refrigerate.

Makes 4 servings

NUTRITIONAL INFORMATION PER SERVING

Calories	198	Saturated Fat (g)	3
Protein (g)	6	Dietary Fiber (g)	9
Carbohydrate (g)	13	Cholesterol (mg)	1
Fat (g)	16	Sodium (mg)	734
Cal. from Fat (%)	65		

Diabetic Exchanges: 1 fruit, 3 fat

BAKED ACORN SQUASH

When this winter squash is in season, here is
an easy very tasty recipe. Just adjust the amounts of sugar
and margarine for how many squash you are preparing.

1	large acorn squash	2	teaspoons margarine
2	tablespoons light brown sugar		

Preheat oven to 350 degrees. Cut squash in half and scoop out seeds and strings; discard. Place in a baking dish filled with ½-inch water, open side up. Bake for 40 minutes. Remove from oven and fill each half with 1 tablespoon brown sugar and 1 teaspoon margarine. Return to oven and continue baking for 10 minutes longer or until tender.

Makes 2 servings

Doc's Notes:

Excellent source of calcium and beta carotene. One cup of acorn squash supplies 90mg of calcium — 11% of the recommended daily allowance.

NUTRITIONAL INFORMATION PER SERVING

Calories	172	Saturated Fat (g)	1
Protein (g)	2	Dietary Fiber (g)	3
Carbohydrate (g)	36	Cholesterol (mg)	0
Fat (g)	4	Sodium (mg)	56
Cal. from Fat (%)	19		

Diabetic Exchanges: 1.5 starch, 1 other carb., 1 fat

NOODLE PUDDING

A plain, slightly sweet dish that makes a nice side dish.

1	(8-ounce) package wide noodles	1	(8-ounce) container nonfat plain yogurt
4	tablespoons margarine, melted	4	ounces light cream cheese
½	cup sugar	3	large egg whites
1	cup low fat cottage cheese	½	teaspoon vanilla extract

Preheat oven to 350 degrees. Boil noodles according to directions on package, omitting oil. Rinse, drain, and combine with margarine, tossing evenly. Place noodles in a glass 13x9x2-inch baking pan coated with nonstick cooking spray. In food processor or mixer, combine remaining ingredients, beating until smooth. Combine with noodles, mixing well. Bake for 45 to 60 minutes.

Makes 15 servings

Doc's Notes:
Excellent source of protein and calcium.

NUTRITIONAL INFORMATION PER SERVING

Calories	150	Saturated Fat (g)	2
Protein (g)	6	Dietary Fiber (g)	0
Carbohydrate (g)	20	Cholesterol (mg)	20
Fat (g)	5	Sodium (mg)	147
Cal. from Fat (%)	30		

Diabetic Exchanges: 0.5 very lean meat, 1 starch, 0.5 other carb., 1 fat

CARROT SOUFFLÉ

Carrots will never have tasted so good!!
Adjust sugar for a less sweet version.

2 pounds carrots, sliced
½ cup sugar
2 large egg whites
3 large eggs
2 tablespoons all-purpose
   flour

1½ teaspoons baking powder
3 tablespoons margarine,
   softened
1 teaspoon vanilla extract

Preheat oven to 350 degrees. Cook carrots in a small amount of water or in the microwave until very soft; drain well. In a mixing bowl, beat carrots. Add sugar, egg whites, and eggs. Mix together flour and baking powder, and add to carrot mixture, blending well. Add margarine and vanilla. Transfer to an oblong baking dish coated with nonstick cooking spray and bake for 1 hour.

Makes 8 servings

Doc's Notes:

Carrots are high in Vitamin C, beta carotene, and potassium. They are also a good source of fiber.

NUTRITIONAL INFORMATION PER SERVING

Calories	176	Saturated Fat (g)	1
Protein (g)	5	Dietary Fiber (g)	4
Carbohydrate (g)	26	Cholesterol (mg)	80
Fat (g)	6	Sodium (mg)	219
Cal. from Fat (%)	32		

Diabetic Exchanges: 2 vegetable, 1 other carb., 1 fat

CREAMED DOUBLE POTATOES

Sweet potatoes are rich in beta carotene and vitamins. This will be easy to tolerate and you are getting valuable nutrition.

1¾ **pounds baking potatoes**	3 **tablespoons margarine**
1¾ **pounds sweet potatoes**	⅓ **cup skim milk**
(yams)	2 **tablespoons honey**

In large pot, cover both types of potatoes with water and boil for 40 minutes or until tender. Peel potatoes and place in mixing bowl with the margarine, blending until smooth. Gradually add the milk and honey, beating until creamy.

Makes 8 servings

Doc's Notes:

Potatoes are rich in Vitamins B6, C, iron, magnesium, niacin, and potassium. Sweet potatoes provide Vitamins A, B6, and C.

NUTRITIONAL INFORMATION PER SERVING

Calories	240	Saturated Fat (g)	1
Protein (g)	4	Dietary Fiber (g)	5
Carbohydrate (g)	47	Cholesterol (mg)	0
Fat (g)	5	Sodium (mg)	74
Cal. from Fat (%)	17		

Diabetic Exchanges: 3 starch, 1 fat

HAM AND CHEESE GRITS QUICHE

Depending on how you feel, be creative with this very tasty recipe by adding sautéed veggies of your choice. This quiche is a nice change for breakfast or for a light meal.

1 cup water	½ cup finely diced ham
⅓ cup dry quick-cooking grits	2 large eggs
1 cup evaporated skim milk	2 large egg whites
1 cup shredded reduced-fat sharp Cheddar cheese	Salt and pepper to taste
	Dash of Worcestershire sauce

Preheat oven to 350 degrees. In a small saucepan, bring the water to a boil; stir in grits. Reduce heat, cover, and cook about 5 minutes or until slightly thickened. In a bowl, combine cooked grits, milk, cheese, ham, eggs, egg whites, salt and pepper, and Worcestershire sauce. Pour mixture into a 9-inch pie plate coated with nonstick cooking spray. Bake for 30 minutes or until set.

Makes 6 servings

NUTRITIONAL INFORMATION PER SERVING

Calories	172	Saturated Fat (g)	3
Protein (g)	16	Dietary Fiber (g)	0
Carbohydrate (g)	12	Cholesterol (mg)	93
Fat (g)	6	Sodium (mg)	216
Cal. from Fat (%)	33		

Diabetic Exchanges: 2 lean meat, 0.5 starch, 0.5 skim milk

QUICK SHRIMP SAUTÉ

In the mood for an easy yet delicious
shrimp dish? Serve over rice or pasta.

2	tablespoons margarine	1	tablespoon Worcestershire
1	bunch green onions		sauce
	(scallions), sliced, optional	1	teaspoon dried basil leaves
1	teaspoon minced garlic	2	cups nonfat plain yogurt
2	pounds raw medium	1	tablespoon all-purpose
	shrimp, peeled		flour

In a large skillet, melt the margarine and sauté the green onions and garlic for two minutes. Add the shrimp, Worcestershire sauce, and basil, cooking until the shrimp are done, about 5 to 7 minutes. Mix the yogurt with the flour and stir into the shrimp mixture and heat thoroughly; do not boil.

Makes 6 servings

Doc's Notes:
This can be chopped or puréed to make it easier to eat.

NUTRITIONAL INFORMATION PER SERVING

Calories	184	Saturated Fat (g)	1
Protein (g)	25	Dietary Fiber (g)	1
Carbohydrate (g)	9	Cholesterol (mg)	181
Fat (g)	5	Sodium (mg)	344
Cal. from Fat (%)	25		

Diabetic Exchanges: 3 very lean meat, 0.5 skim milk, 0.5 fat

GERMAN CHOCOLATE ANGEL PIE

Easy, refreshing fabulous dessert, make ahead and freeze. Easy to swallow as it melts in your mouth.

3   large egg whites, room
    temperature
¼   teaspoon salt
¼   teaspoon cream of tartar
¾   cup sugar
1   tablespoon plus 1 teaspoon
    vanilla extract, divided

1   (4-ounce) bar German
    Sweet Chocolate
3   tablespoons water
1   (8-ounce) container fat-free
    frozen whipped topping,
    thawed

Preheat oven to 300 degrees. Beat egg whites with salt and cream of tartar until foamy. Add sugar, 2 tablespoons at a time, beating well after each addition. Continue beating until stiff peaks form. Fold in 1 tablespoon vanilla. Spoon into 9-inch lightly greased glass pie plate and form nest-like shell. Bake 45 minutes. Cool. In a microwave safe bowl, melt chocolate in water for 1 minute, stir until melted. Cool. Add remaining 1 teaspoon vanilla. Fold whipped topping into cooled chocolate. Spoon into meringue shell. Freeze. Thaw slightly to serve.

Makes 8 servings

NUTRITIONAL INFORMATION PER SERVING

Calories	198	Saturated Fat (g)	2
Protein (g)	2	Dietary Fiber (g)	1
Carbohydrate (g)	37	Cholesterol (mg)	0
Fat (g)	4	Sodium (mg)	109
Cal. from Fat (%)	17		

Diabetic Exchanges: 2.5 other carb., 1 fat

CREAM CHEESE BREAD PUDDING

*Bread pudding is always a popular dessert, but with
the cream cheese topping it reaches new heights! If having
trouble swallowing, use regular bread and cut off the crusts.*

1	(16-ounce) loaf French bread	1	teaspoon imitation butter flavoring
2	large eggs, divided	3	cups skim milk
4	large egg whites, divided	1	teaspoon ground cinnamon
1	cup sugar, divided	1	(8-ounce) package fat-free cream cheese, softened
1	teaspoon vanilla extract		

Preheat oven to 350 degrees. Cut the French bread into 1-inch squares. Place the bread in a 13x9x2-inch baking dish. In a large bowl, lightly beat together 1 egg and 3 egg whites. Add ½ cup sugar, vanilla, and butter flavoring; mix well. Slowly add the milk to the egg mixture, mixing well. Pour over the bread squares. Sprinkle the mixture with the cinnamon. In a large mixing bowl, beat the cream cheese with the remaining ½ cup sugar. Add the remaining egg and egg white, blending until smooth. Spread the mixture evenly over the soaked bread. Bake, uncovered, for 45 minutes or until firm. Let cool slightly before serving.

Makes 8 servings

Doc's Notes:
Another good source of calcium and protein.

NUTRITIONAL INFORMATION PER SERVING

Calories	340	Saturated Fat (g)	1
Protein (g)	16	Dietary Fiber (g)	2
Carbohydrate (g)	62	Cholesterol (mg)	57
Fat (g)	3	Sodium (mg)	573
Cal. from Fat (%)	8		

Diabetic Exchanges: 1 very lean meat, 2 starch, 0.5 skim milk, 1.5 other carb.

STRAWBERRY WEIGHT GAIN SHAKE

Try placing the shake in freezer trays. Freeze 1½ hours
or serve in a glass and stir until desired consistency.

1 (8-ounce) can vanilla
   nutritional energy drink
   supplement, chilled

1 cup frozen strawberries
   (unsweetened)
2 teaspoons sugar

Place supplement and strawberries in a blender. Add sugar and blend until smooth.

Makes 1 serving

Doc's Notes:

A good source of Vitamin C, potassium, and extra calories. A great way to hide the nutritional supplement

NUTRITIONAL INFORMATION PER SERVING

Calories	320	Saturated Fat (g)	0
Protein (g)	11	Dietary Fiber (g)	3
Carbohydrate (g)	62	Cholesterol (mg)	0
Fat (g)	4	Sodium (mg)	131
Cal. from Fat (%)	12		

Diabetic Exchanges: 2.5 starch, 1 fruit, 0.5 other carb., 0.5 fat

AWESOME MILK SHAKE

Nothing beats a cold shake! Vary the recipe to get extra calories.
Add various flavors to create different kinds of shakes.

½ cup skim milk
2 cups frozen nonfat vanilla yogurt or fat-free ice cream

1 teaspoon vanilla extract
3 tablespoons chocolate syrup, optional

In a blender or food processor, place the milk, frozen yogurt, and vanilla and blend until smooth. If you want a chocolate milk shake, add the chocolate syrup to the mixture

Makes 2 servings

Doc's Notes:

If you need calories, use regular ice cream and replace the skim milk with a vanilla nutritional energy drink supplement. For different shakes, use different flavors of ice cream and delete the chocolate syrup if it doesn't fit in.

NUTRITIONAL INFORMATION PER SERVING

Calories 218
Protein (g) 12
Carbohydrate (g) 41
Fat (g) 0
Cal. from Fat (%) 0
Saturated Fat (g) 0
Dietary Fiber (g) 0
Cholesterol (mg) 4
Sodium (mg) 160

Diabetic Exchanges: 0.5 skim milk, 2.5 other carb.

SNACKS AND LIGHT MEALS

✦ *Is snacking permissible?*
✦ *Should I make snacks ahead of time?*

Snacking is not only permissible but strongly encouraged. It is sometimes very hard to sit down for a full five-course meal, but easier to sit down to a thirty minute meal with two to three snacks in between. High calorie, low volume snacks are important to help you to maintain your weight. We will try to offer suggestions for snacks that can be made easily and with minimal effort.

STRAWBERRY SLUSH

Absolutely yummy! You will repeat this
recipe often as it is so soothing to drink.

1 cup fresh strawberries, hulled and halved	½ cup orange juice
2 tablespoons sugar	1 tablespoon lemon juice

Combine all ingredients in a blender or food processor and process until smooth.

Makes 1 serving

Doc's Notes:

Get your extra potassium and Vitamin C from these strawberries. If white blood cell count is low, don't use raw fruit.

NUTRITIONAL INFORMATION PER SERVING

Calories	202	Saturated Fat (g)	0
Protein (g)	2	Dietary Fiber (g)	4
Carbohydrate (g)	50	Cholesterol (mg)	0
Fat (g)	1	Sodium (mg)	3
Cal. from Fat (%)	3		

Diabetic Exchanges: 2 fruit, 1.5 other carb.

CEREAL MIXTURE

Double this recipe and store in a jar. Great snack for everyone.

3 tablespoons honey	3 cups cereal (assorted
3 tablespoon margarine	shredded wheat, corn
3 tablespoons reduced-fat	bran chex)
peanut butter	

Preheat oven to 175 degrees. In the microwave, combine honey, margarine, and peanut butter and heat until smooth. Toss with cereal, coating well. Spread on a baking sheet and bake for 1½ hours.

Makes six (½-cup) servings

Doc's Notes:
Keep this on hand for daily snacking. Every calorie counts. Peanut butter adds protein and the cereal adds fiber, vitamins, and minerals.

NUTRITIONAL INFORMATION PER SERVING

Calories	201	Saturated Fat (g)	2
Protein (g)	5	Dietary Fiber (g)	4
Carbohydrate (g)	30	Cholesterol (mg)	0
Fat (g)	9	Sodium (mg)	199
Cal. from Fat (%)	37		

Diabetic Exchanges: 1.5 starch, 0.5 other carb., 1.5 fat

SNACK MIX

Here's an easy recipe that makes a great snack mix
any time of day. Sweet and salty mixes are always
a great combo and this mix is addicting!

3	tablespoons sesame oil	6	cups mini pretzels
3	tablespoons honey	1	cup soy nuts
1	tablespoon soy sauce	1	cup dry roasted peanuts
½	teaspoon garlic salt	1	cup candy-coated chocolate
½	teaspoon onion powder		pieces
4	cups crispy wheat cereal squares		

Preheat oven to 250 degrees. Whisk together sesame oil, honey, soy sauce, garlic salt, and onion powder. Toss together cereal squares, pretzels, soy nuts, and peanuts in a large bowl. Drizzle oil mixture over cereal mixture, tossing gently to coat. Scatter mixture on a foil-lined jelly roll pan and bake for 25 minutes, stirring often to prevent too much browning. Turn off oven and let cereal stay in oven for 1 hour to continue crisping. When cool, toss with the chocolate candies. Store in an airtight container for up to one week.

Makes twenty (½-cup) servings

Doc's Notes:
Add one cup of raisins for extra iron.

NUTRITIONAL INFORMATION PER SERVING

Calories	242	Saturated Fat (g)	3
Protein (g)	8	Dietary Fiber (g)	3
Carbohydrate (g)	32	Cholesterol (mg)	2
Fat (g)	10	Sodium (mg)	400
Cal. from Fat (%)	37		

Diabetic Exchanges: 0.5 very lean meat, 1 starch, 1 other carb., 2 fat

CORNMEAL FRUITY SNACK MUFFINS

These grainy fruit muffins make a perfect snack during the day. Add nuts if desired and you can substitute fresh fruit such as blueberries. Store in zip lock bags.

2 cups all-purpose flour	½ cup unsweetened applesauce
1 cup yellow cornmeal	2 large eggs
⅓ cup sugar	1 large egg white
1½ teaspoons baking powder	1 teaspoon grated orange rind
1 teaspoon baking soda	3 cups assorted dried fruit
1 teaspoon ground cinnamon	(raisins, cranberries, mixed
1¾ cups buttermilk	fruit)
⅓ cup canola oil	

Preheat oven to 400 degrees. In large bowl, mix flour, cornmeal, sugar, baking powder, baking soda, and cinnamon. Stir in buttermilk, oil, applesauce, eggs, egg white, and orange rind, mixing. Gently stir in dried fruit. Spoon batter into paper-lined muffin tins. Bake about 18 minutes or until toothpick inserted comes out clean.

Makes 24 muffins

Doc's Notes:
The dried fruit adds the extra fiber needed to keep you regular.

NUTRITIONAL INFORMATION PER SERVING

Calories	155	Saturated Fat (g)	1
Protein (g)	3	Dietary Fiber (g)	2
Carbohydrate (g)	28	Cholesterol (mg)	18
Fat (g)	4	Sodium (mg)	113
Cal. from Fat (%)	22		

Diabetic Exchanges: 1 starch, 1 fruit, 1 fat

CINNAMON QUICK BREAD

*A quick bread that will appeal at all
times as it's not too rich but very tasty.*

2 cups all-purpose flour	2 large eggs
1 teaspoon baking powder	1 teaspoon vanilla extract
1 teaspoon baking soda	1 cup buttermilk
½ cup margarine	1½ teaspoons ground
1 cup plus 1 tablespoon	cinnamon
sugar, divided	

Preheat oven to 350 degrees. In bowl combine flour, baking powder, and baking soda; set aside. In another mixing bowl, blend margarine and 1 cup sugar. Gradually add eggs and vanilla. Stir in flour mixture and buttermilk alternately, mixing until smooth. Transfer half the batter into a 9x5x3-inch loaf pan coated with nonstick cooking spray. In another small bowl mix together remaining 1 tablespoon sugar and cinnamon. Sprinkle a light dusting over the batter. Swirl the cinnamon sugar into the layer of batter with a knife. Cover with remaining batter and cinnamon sugar. For a crusted effect, don't swirl the top mixture, lightly dust it over the batter. Bake for 50 to 60 minutes or until a toothpick inserted comes out clean.

Makes 16 servings

NUTRITIONAL INFORMATION PER SERVING

Calories	176	Saturated Fat (g)	1
Protein (g)	3	Dietary Fiber (g)	1
Carbohydrate (g)	26	Cholesterol (mg)	27
Fat (g)	7	Sodium (mg)	200
Cal. from Fat (%)	33		

Diabetic Exchanges: 1 starch, 0.5 other carb., 1 fat

SPINACH DIP

Whichever way you eat this wonderful dip, it will be with a smile. Spread on French bread halves and bake in the oven for wonderful Spinach Bread. Makes a great side veggie dish, also.

2 (10-ounce) packages frozen chopped spinach
½ cup chopped onion
2 tablespoons all-purpose flour

1 (12-ounce) can evaporated skimmed milk
Salt and pepper to taste
½ teaspoon garlic powder
1 cup shredded part-skim mozzarella cheese

Preheat oven to 350 degrees. Prepare spinach according to the package directions; drain well. In a small saucepan coated with nonstick cooking spray, sauté the onion over medium heat 5 minutes or until tender. Add the cooked spinach and flour. Gradually stir in milk, salt, pepper, and garlic powder. Cook over medium-high heat until thickened and bubbly. Remove from the heat. Add the mozzarella cheese, stirring just until mixed.

Makes twelve (¼-cup) servings

Doc's Notes:
This is a great source of potassium.

NUTRITIONAL INFORMATION PER SERVING

Calories 68
Protein (g) 6
Carbohydrate (g) 7
Fat (g) 2
Cal. from Fat (%) 22

Saturated Fat (g) 1
Dietary Fiber (g) 2
Cholesterol (mg) 7
Sodium (mg) 116

Diabetic Exchanges: 0.5 lean meat, 0.5 skim milk

STRAWBERRY FRUIT DIP

Also makes a sensational soup or smoothie.

1   quart strawberries, stemmed and finely chopped
¼   cup light brown sugar

¼   cup orange juice
1   cup nonfat vanilla yogurt
½   teaspoon grated orange rind

In a bowl, mix all ingredients. Cover and refrigerate.

Makes 40 (1-tablespoon) servings

Doc's Notes:
High in Vitamin C. Avoid fresh fruit if low white blood cell count.

NUTRITIONAL INFORMATION PER SERVING

Calories	16	Saturated Fat (g)	0
Protein (g)	0	Dietary Fiber (g)	0
Carbohydrate (g)	4	Cholesterol (mg)	0
Fat (g)	0	Sodium (mg)	5
Cal. from Fat (%)	0		

Diabetic Exchanges: Free

FRESH FRUIT DIP

Great dip and nothing could be faster.

2   (8-ounce) cartons low-fat lemon yogurt
¼   cup blanched almonds, chopped and toasted

1   teaspoon grated orange rind
2   tablespoons orange juice

Combine the lemon yogurt, almonds, orange rind, and orange juice and mix well. Refrigerate. Keeps in refrigerator 1 week.

Makes eight (¼-cup) servings

Doc's Notes:
Yogurt is an excellent source of calcium and protein, and a good source of riboflavin, phosphorus and Vitamin B12.

NUTRITIONAL INFORMATION PER SERVING

Calories	88	Saturated Fat (g)	1
Protein (g)	4	Dietary Fiber (g)	1
Carbohydrate (g)	10	Cholesterol (mg)	3
Fat (g)	3	Sodium (mg)	38
Cal. from Fat (%)	30		

Diabetic Exchanges: 0.5 skim milk, 0.5 fat

STRAWBERRY SALSA

*A great dip or compliment to whatever
you serve such as chicken or fish.*

2 cups strawberries
½ cup chopped green bell
    peppers
2 tablespoons chopped red
    onion
2 tablespoons chopped
    parsley

2 tablespoons raspberry
    vinegar
1 tablespoon canola oil
1 tablespoon honey
Dash of hot pepper sauce,
    optional
Tortilla chips

In a bowl, combine strawberries, green pepper, onions, and parsley. In a separate bowl, combine vinegar, oil, honey, and hot sauce. Toss with strawberry mixture. Cover and refrigerate for 2 hours. Serve with tortilla chips.

Makes eight (¼-cup) servings

Doc's Notes:
Not only is this delicious it is also a good source of Vitamin C and potassium.

NUTRITIONAL INFORMATION PER SERVING

Calories	38	Saturated Fat (g)	0
Protein (g)	0	Dietary Fiber (g)	1
Carbohydrate (g)	6	Cholesterol (mg)	0
Fat (g)	2	Sodium (mg)	1
Cal. from Fat (%)	41		

Diabetic Exchanges: 0.5 fruit, 0.5 fat

ARTICHOKE SQUARES

Great served warm, room temperature, or cold, and very appealing.

1 cup green onions (scallions)	½ teaspoon dried oregano leaves
1 teaspoon minced garlic	
2 cups sliced mushrooms	2 large eggs
1 (2-ounce) jar diced pimentos, drained	3 large egg whites
	¾ cup Italian bread crumbs
2 (14-ounce) cans artichoke hearts, drained and chopped	1 cup shredded reduced-fat Swiss cheese
	1 cup shredded reduced-fat Cheddar cheese
¼ cup chopped parsley	Salt and pepper to taste

Preheat oven to 350 degrees. In pan coated with nonstick cooking spray, sauté onion, garlic, and mushrooms until tender. In a bowl, combine onion mixture, pimentos, artichoke hearts, parsley, oregano, egg, egg whites, bread crumbs, cheeses, salt and pepper, mixing well. Pour into a 13x9x2-inch baking dish coated with nonstick cooking spray and bake for 30 minutes or until mixture is set. Cut into squares.

Makes 35 squares

Doc's Notes:

Artichokes provide Vitamin C, folacin, magnesium, phosphorus, and potassium. Mushrooms provide B Vitamins, copper, and other minerals.

NUTRITIONAL INFORMATION PER SERVING

Calories 43
Protein (g) 3   Dietary Fiber (g) 1
Carbohydrate (g) 3   Cholesterol (mg) 16
Fat (g) 2   Sodium (mg) 137
Cal. from Fat (%) 37
Saturated Fat (g) 1

Diabetic Exchanges: 0.5 lean meat

ITALIAN PASTA SALAD

This vegetarian salad can be adjusted to your taste and your pantry.
Use your imagination and your favorite kind of pasta.

8 ounces ziti pasta	2 Roma (plum) tomatoes, chopped
4 ounces tri-colored rotini	½ cup red wine vinegar
1 green bell pepper, cored and chopped	¼ cup water
1 red bell pepper, cored and chopped	1 teaspoon dried basil leaves
½ cup chopped celery	1 teaspoon dried oregano leaves
2 teaspoons drained capers	½ teaspoon minced garlic
⅓ cup thinly sliced green onions (scallions)	1 tablespoon Dijon mustard
	¼ cup grated Parmesan cheese

Cook both the pastas together according to package directions, omitting the oil and salt. Rinse and drain and place in a large bowl. Add the bell peppers, celery, capers, green onions, and tomatoes. Combine the vinegar with the water, basil, oregano, garlic, mustard, and Parmesan cheese in a small bowl, mixing well. Pour over the pasta mixture and toss well.

Makes 8 to 12 servings

Doc's Notes:

Pasta is rich in complex carbohydrates, high in protein, low in fat and delicious.

NUTRITIONAL INFORMATION PER SERVING

Calories	127	Saturated Fat (g)	1
Protein (g)	5	Dietary Fiber (g)	1
Carbohydrate (g)	24	Cholesterol (mg)	2
Fat (g)	1	Sodium (mg)	96
Cal. from Fat (%)	8		

Diabetic Exchanges: 1.5 starch

MINI CHEESE PIZZAS

These are easy to make and are super for a quick snack or lunch.

1 **(10-biscuit) can flaky refrigerated biscuits**
⅓ **cup tomato sauce**

½ **teaspoon dried oregano leaves**
½ **cup shredded part-skim Mozzarella cheese**

Preheat oven to 450 degrees. Pat each biscuit into a 4-inch circle on a baking sheet coated with nonstick cooking spray. In a small bowl, mix together the tomato sauce and oregano. Spoon the sauce on each biscuit round. Sprinkle the cheese over the tomato sauce. Bake for 8 to 10 minutes or until the cheese is melted.

Makes 10 pizzas

Doc's Notes:
Add appealing veggies for extra nutrition.

NUTRITIONAL INFORMATION PER SERVING

Calories	117	Saturated Fat (g)	2
Protein (g)	4	Dietary Fiber (g)	0
Carbohydrate (g)	15	Cholesterol (mg)	3
Fat (g)	5	Sodium (mg)	424
Cal. from Fat (%)	40		

Diabetic Exchanges: 1 starch, 1 fat

FRESH TOMATO
AND CHEESE PIZZA

Simply tomato and cheese, yet interesting enough to enjoy.

2   thin slices red onion, cut in half
2   cloves garlic, thinly sliced
1   (10-ounce) can refrigerated pizza crust dough or Boboli prepared crust
1   (15-ounce) carton nonfat ricotta cheese
1   cup shredded part-skim mozzarella cheese
¼   cup grated Parmesan cheese, divided
1   tablespoon dried basil leaves
4   Roma (plum) tomatoes, thinly sliced

Preheat the broiler. Place the onion and garlic on a baking sheet coated with nonstick cooking spray. Broil 6 inches from the heat 8 to 10 minutes, or until charred; set aside. Change oven setting to bake at 450 degrees. Roll the dough into a 12-inch circle and press into a pizza pan coated with nonstick cooking spray. Combine the ricotta cheese, mozzarella cheese, Parmesan cheese, and basil, stirring well. Spread the cheese over the dough, leaving a ½-inch border. Arrange the tomato slices over the cheese. Top with the onion and garlic. Bake on the bottom rack of the oven for 10 to 12 minutes, or until the crust is browned. Transfer the pizza to a cutting board.

Makes 8 slices

Doc's Notes:

Italian food seems to be a favorite among patients receiving chemotherapy. As long as your mouth is not sore and your white blood cell count is not low, enjoy! The cheese provides protein and calcium while the tomatoes are rich in vitamins A and C.

NUTRITIONAL INFORMATION PER SERVING

Calories	184	Saturated Fat (g)	2
Protein (g)	15	Dietary Fiber (g)	1
Carbohydrate (g)	20	Cholesterol (mg)	15
Fat (g)	5	Sodium (mg)	445
Cal. from Fat (%)	22		

Diabetic Exchanges: 1.5 lean meat, 1 starch, 1 vegetable

ASPARAGUS AND BRIE PIZZA

By using asparagus and brie you turn
this ordinary pizza into something special.

12 thin asparagus spears, tips only
1   red bell pepper, cored and thinly sliced, optional
1   teaspoon minced garlic
1   (10-ounce) can refrigerated pizza crust or 1 (16-ounce) Boboli prepared crust
½   teaspoon dried basil leaves
½   teaspoon dried oregano leaves
Salt and pepper to taste
3½ ounces Brie cheese, skin removed and thinly sliced

Preheat oven to 425 degrees. Fill in small saucepan with water and bring to a boil. Cook the asparagus tips until tender, about 4 minutes. Drain and set aside. Heat a skillet coated with nonstick cooking spray over medium heat and sauté the bell pepper until tender, about 4 minutes. Blend in the garlic. Coat a 12-inch pizza pan with nonstick cooking spray. Unroll the dough and place in the prepared pan, starting at the center and pressing out with your hands. Bake for 5 minutes. Remove and sprinkle the crust with the basil, oregano, and salt and pepper, if desired, then evenly distribute the Brie cheese, bell pepper, and asparagus on top. Bake for 8 to 10 minutes more.

Makes 8 slices

Doc's Notes:

Asparagus is rich in Vitamins A, B6, C, and E. It also has a high content of folacin.

NUTRITIONAL INFORMATION PER SERVING

Calories	133	Saturated Fat (g)	2
Protein (g)	6	Dietary Fiber (g)	1
Carbohydrate (g)	17	Cholesterol (mg)	12
Fat (g)	5	Sodium (mg)	294
Cal. from Fat (%)	31		

Diabetic Exchanges: 0.5 lean meat, 1 starch, 0.5 fat

SPINACH AND CHEESE TORTILLA PIZZA

By using tortillas, this is an easy yet satisfying meal.

2 large (10-inch) flour tortillas
2 tablespoons nonfat plain yogurt
1 (10-ounce) package frozen chopped spinach, thawed and squeezed dry
1 large tomato, chopped
½ cup shredded reduced-fat Monterey Jack cheese
¼ cup thinly sliced green onions (scallions)

Preheat oven to 450 degrees. Place the tortillas on a baking sheet coated with nonstick cooking spray. Bake for 3 minutes, or until golden brown. Remove from the oven and reduce the temperature to 350 degrees. Spread the yogurt evenly over the tortillas. Top with the spinach and tomato. Next, sprinkle evenly with the Monterey Jack cheese. Bake for 5 minutes more, or until the cheese is melted. Sprinkle with the green onions. Cut each tortilla into 6 slices and serve immediately.

Makes 12 slices

Doc's Notes:
You will have to fight your family for these. Spinach is a great source of beta carotene and folate.

NUTRITIONAL INFORMATION PER SERVING

Calories	64	Saturated Fat (g)	1
Protein (g)	3	Dietary Fiber (g)	1
Carbohydrate (g)	9	Cholesterol (mg)	3
Fat (g)	2	Sodium (mg)	108
Cal. from Fat (%)	25		

Diabetic Exchanges: 0.5 starch

CHEESE QUESADILLAS

Add sautéed veggies or keep it simple
with cheese for this simple snack or meal.

2 (8-inch) flour tortillas   Taco sauce
½ cup shredded reduced-fat
    Cheddar or Monterey Jack
    cheese

In a pan coated with nonstick cooking spray, on a low heat, place one flour tortilla. Sprinkle with the cheese and top with the other flour tortilla. Cook about 1 to 1½ minutes on each side turning with a spatula. Coat the pan again with nonstick cooking spray before turning over. Make sure the cheese is melted and the tortillas are light brown. Watch carefully and cook slowly over a low heat to allow the cheese to melt. Cut into wedges and serve with taco sauce.

Makes 6 slices

NUTRITIONAL INFORMATION PER SERVING

Calories 80
Protein (g) 4
Carbohydrate (g) 9
Fat (g) 3
Cal. from Fat (%) 33

Saturated Fat (g) 2
Dietary Fiber (g) 1
Cholesterol (mg) 5
Sodium (mg) 138

Diabetic Exchanges: 0.5 lean meat, 0.5 starch

ITALIAN SPINACH PIE

A quiche like pie that makes a light meal.

½ cup chopped onions
2 (10-ounce) packages frozen chopped spinach
1 (14½-ounce) can artichoke hearts, quartered
1 cup fat-free ricotta cheese
¼ cup skim milk
2 large egg whites, beaten with a fork
½ teaspoon garlic powder
1 (8-ounce) can no-salt added tomato sauce
½ teaspoon dried oregano leaves
½ teaspoon dried basil leaves
½ cup shredded part-skim mozzarella cheese

Preheat oven to 350 degrees. In a skillet coated with nonstick cooking spray, sauté the onions over medium heat until tender, about 5 minutes. Meanwhile, cook the spinach according to package directions; drain very well. In a large bowl, combine the onions, spinach, artichoke hearts, ricotta cheese, milk, egg whites, and garlic powder, mixing well. Spoon the mixture into a 9-inch pie plate coated with nonstick cooking spray. Mix the tomato sauce with the oregano and basil and spread evenly over the spinach. Bake for 15 minutes. Sprinkle with the mozzarella cheese and bake for 5 to 10 minutes longer, until the cheese is melted.

Makes 6 servings

Doc's Notes:

Spinach provides potassium while the tomatoes add vitamins A and C, folacin, magnesium, phosphorus, and potassium.

NUTRITIONAL INFORMATION PER SERVING

Calories 116
Protein (g) 14
Carbohydrate (g) 12
Fat (g) 2
Cal. from Fat (%) 14
Saturated Fat (g) 1
Dietary Fiber (g) 4
Cholesterol (mg) 9
Sodium (mg) 342

Diabetic Exchanges: 1.5 very lean meat, 2 vegetable

SOUTHWESTERN STUFFED POTATOES

This variation is a great choice if you enjoy stuffed potatoes. Make a bunch and freeze for a quick lunch.

3 medium baking potatoes	1 (4-ounce) can diced green chiles, optional
3 tablespoons margarine	
2 tablespoons skim milk	4 green onions (scallions), chopped
½ cup nonfat plain yogurt	
1 (17-ounce) can whole kernel corn, drained	1 cup shredded reduced-fat Cheddar cheese
	Paprika

Preheat oven to 400 degrees. Wash potatoes well, and dry thoroughly. With fork, prick skins over entire surface. Place potatoes directly on oven rack, and bake for about 1 hour or until soft when squeezed. When done, cut each potato in half lengthwise. Scoop out inside, leaving a thin shell. In mixer, mash potato pulp until no lumps remain. Add margarine, skim milk, and yogurt, mixing well. Stir in corn, green chiles, green onions, and cheese, combining well. Spoon mixture into shells. Top with paprika. Lower oven to 350 degrees and bake for about 20 minutes or until cheese is melted and potatoes are hot.

Makes 6 servings

NUTRITIONAL INFORMATION PER SERVING

Calories	228	Saturated Fat (g)	3
Protein (g)	11	Dietary Fiber (g)	4
Carbohydrate (g)	29	Cholesterol (mg)	11
Fat (g)	10	Sodium (mg)	422
Cal. from Fat (%)	36		

Diabetic Exchanges: 1 lean meat, 2 starch, 1 fat

COFFEE CAKE

This cake will definitely be a hit for all those coffee cake lovers.

1 (8-ounce) tub margarine	1 teaspoon imitation butter
1¼ cups sugar	flavoring
2 cups nonfat plain yogurt	3 cups all-purpose flour
3 large egg whites	1½ teaspoons baking powder
1 teaspoon vanilla extract	1 teaspoon baking soda

Preheat oven to 350 degrees. In mixing bowl, beat margarine and sugar until fluffy. Add yogurt, egg whites, vanilla, and butter flavoring, mixing well. Combine flour, baking powder, and baking soda together. Gradually add to yogurt mixture, mixing well. Pour one third of the batter into a 10-inch Bundt pan coated with nonstick cooking spray and dusted with flour. Sprinkle with half the Nut Filling (recipe follows). Repeat layers, ending with batter. Bake for 55 minutes or until toothpick inserted in center of cake comes out clean.

Nut Filling

½ cup light brown sugar	½ cup chopped pecans
1½ teaspoons ground cinnamon	

In a small bowl, combine all ingredients. Mix with fork until crumbly.

Makes 24 servings

NUTRITIONAL INFORMATION PER SERVING

Calories 214	Saturated Fat (g) 2
Protein (g) 4	Dietary Fiber (g) 1
Carbohydrate (g) 29	Cholesterol (mg) 0
Fat (g) 9	Sodium (mg) 179
Cal. from Fat (%) 39	

Diabetic Exchanges: 1 starch, 1 other carb., 1.5 fat

NO BAKE COOKIES

These ingredients are always in the pantry.
A quick and nourishing cure for a sweet tooth.

½ **cup graham cracker crumbs**
2½ **cups old fashioned oatmeal**
1½ **cups sugar**
2 **tablespoons cocoa**
½ **cup skim milk**

½ **cup margarine**
½ **cup reduced-fat peanut butter**
1 **teaspoon vanilla extract**

In a bowl, combine graham cracker crumbs and oatmeal. Set aside. In a saucepan, stir sugar, cocoa, milk, and margarine over medium heat until dissolved. Bring mixture to a boil and cook for 2 minutes. Remove from heat. Stir in peanut butter and vanilla until well combined. Quickly blend in cracker mixture. Beat by hand for a few minutes or until thickened. Drop by teaspoonfuls onto waxed paper. Refrigerate until firm and store in refrigerator.

Makes 5 dozen

Doc's Notes:

These cookies are a good source of fiber and protein. Peanuts are a good source of thiamin, niacin, folacin, iron, and magnesium.

NUTRITIONAL INFORMATION PER SERVING

Calories	62	Saturated Fat (g)	0
Protein (g)	1	Dietary Fiber (g)	1
Carbohydrate (g)	9	Cholesterol (mg)	0
Fat (g)	3	Sodium (mg)	37
Cal. from Fat (%)	36		

Diabetic Exchanges: 0.5 starch, 0.5 fat

YUMMY COOKIES

*Yummy cookies loaded with oatmeal and
peanut butter and a treat of chocolate.*

½	cup margarine	1	teaspoon vanilla extract
½	cup sugar	1	cup all-purpose flour
1	cup brown sugar	1	teaspoon baking soda
1	large egg	4	cups old fashioned oatmeal
1	cup reduced-fat crunchy peanut butter	½	cup chocolate chips, optional

Preheat oven to 350 degrees. In a mixing bowl, cream margarine, sugar, and brown sugar. Add egg; mixing well. Add peanut butter and vanilla. Combine flour and baking soda; add to creamed mixture. Stir in oatmeal and chocolate chips. Spoon batter by teaspoonfuls onto a baking sheet. Bake for 10 to 12 minutes or until done.

Makes 4½ dozen cookies

NUTRITIONAL INFORMATION PER SERVING

Calories	94	Saturated Fat (g)	1
Protein (g)	3	Dietary Fiber (g)	1
Carbohydrate (g)	13	Cholesterol (mg)	4
Fat (g)	4	Sodium (mg)	72
Cal. from Fat (%)	35		

Diabetic Exchanges: 0.5 starch, 0.5 other carb., 0.5 fat

MOCHA MERINGUE MOUNDS

Meringues with lots of personality! These are easy to tolerate.

3	large egg whites	½	teaspoon vanilla extract
	Dash of salt	½	cup mini semisweet
½	cup sugar		chocolate chips
1	tablespoon instant coffee		

Preheat oven to 300 degrees. In a large mixing bowl, beat egg whites with dash of salt at high speed of mixer for one minute. Mix sugar with instant coffee, and gradually add sugar mixture, 1 tablespoon at a time, beating 3 minutes or until stiff peaks form and sugar mixture is dissolved. Beat in vanilla. Gently fold in chocolate chips. Drop by heaping teaspoonfuls onto a baking sheet lined with wax paper. Bake for 30 minutes. Cool slightly on baking sheet before removing.

Makes 3 dozen meringue mounds

NUTRITIONAL INFORMATION PER SERVING

Calories	24	Saturated Fat (g)	0
Protein (g)	0	Dietary Fiber (g)	0
Carbohydrate (g)	4	Cholesterol (mg)	0
Fat (g)	1	Sodium (mg)	5
Cal. from Fat (%)	25		

Diabetic Exchanges: 0.5 other carb.

CAREGIVER

◈ *Should frozen dishes be brought over?*

◈ *Are snacks a good idea?*

There is nothing more comforting when you are sick than an act of kindness from a friend. Sometimes patients do not want to discuss their appetite or their situation. Being there to listen and offer a warm smile is often the greatest gift. A thoughtful snack, casserole, or other healthy dish can bring joy and happiness to a loved one. This can also be helpful for family members or caregivers.

Even the smell of cooking can upset your stomach at times. Patients tell me that often they have their food prepared in an outside kitchen to avoid the aroma. Having a surprise will sometimes entice you to eat. We will try to offer recipes for foods and drinks that can be heated, defrosted, or served with minimal preparation. A real treat is to include paper plates, forks and spoons so you do not have to worry about washing dishes and your meal really is ready to eat. Try to keep it simple and inviting. Eating with a friend or family can also be very helpful. It is no fun to eat alone.

What Can People Do To Help?
◈ Encourage and support without being overwhelming.
◈ Accompany you to the grocery store.
◈ Take your list and go shopping for you.
◈ Help you to prepare food.
◈ Help organize ready-to-eat snacks.
◈ Organize friends/or relatives to cook for you and your family.
◈ Meals should be brought over in disposable containers.
◈ Run errands for you.
◈ Eat with you.
◈ Take you for a ride.
◈ Read to you.
◈ Give the caregiver a break.

BANANA BREAD

I hate the thought of throwing bananas away so when I have ripe bananas I always make a banana bread and stick it in my freezer to pull out or bring to a friend. For added calories and taste, add some chocolate chips or butterscotch chips.

⅓	cup canola oil	1	teaspoon vanilla extract
1	cup dark brown sugar	2	cups all-purpose flour
2	large eggs	1	teaspoon baking soda
3	medium bananas, mashed	1	teaspoon ground cinnamon

Preheat oven to 350 degrees. In a mixing bowl, beat together the oil and brown sugar. Add eggs, banana, and vanilla. In a separate bowl, combine flour, baking soda and cinnamon. Gradually add the dry ingredients, stirring until mixed. Pour batter into a 9x5x3-inch loaf pan coated with nonstick cooking spray. Bake 50 to 60 minutes or until a toothpick inserted in the center comes out clean.

Makes 16 slices

Doc's Notes:

Banana Bread is great for an afternoon snack or a light breakfast. The bananas are a good food to consume if diarrhea is a problem. Each banana has about 450 mg of potassium.

NUTRITIONAL INFORMATION PER SERVING

Calories	180	Saturated Fat (g)	1
Protein (g)	3	Dietary Fiber (g)	1
Carbohydrate (g)	31	Cholesterol (mg)	27
Fat (g)	5	Sodium (mg)	93
Cal. from Fat (%)	27		

Diabetic Exchanges: 1 starch, 0.5 fruit, 0.5 other carb., 1 fat

SPINACH LAYERED DISH

Prepare the night before to enjoy the next day for brunch or a light dinner. Spinach and a light red sauce layered with cheese.

½ pound mushrooms, sliced
1 onion, chopped
1 teaspoon minced garlic, divided
1 (10-ounce) package frozen chopped spinach, thawed and squeezed dry
1 (28-ounce) can crushed tomatoes with their juice
1 teaspoon dried oregano leaves
12 slices Italian bread, crusts removed
1 (8-ounce) package part-skim Mozzarella cheese, shredded
4 large eggs
4 large egg whites
2 cups skim milk

In a medium skillet coated with nonstick cooking spray, sauté the mushrooms, onion, and ½ teaspoon garlic until tender, about 3 to 5 minutes. Add the spinach, mixing well; set aside. In a small bowl, mix together the tomatoes, oregano, and remaining ½ teaspoon garlic. Spread about 1 cup of the tomato sauce along the bottom of a 3-quart casserole dish coated with nonstick cooking spray. Top with 6 slices of the bread. Cover the bread evenly with half of the spinach mixture, half the cheese, and another 1 cup of the sauce. Repeat the layers with the remaining bread, spinach, cheese, and sauce. In a separate bowl or in a food processor, whisk or blend together the eggs, egg whites and skim milk. Pour the egg mixture slowly over the casserole until the mixture has been absorbed. Cover and refrigerate for 6 hours or overnight. Preheat oven to 350 degrees. Place the casserole in the oven and bake for 1 hour or until all the egg mixture is done.

Makes 10 to 12 servings

Doc's Notes:

The tomatoes may be a little rough on a sore mouth, but if your mouth feels good, enjoy. Eggs provide a good source of high quality protein and are an important source of Vitamins B12 and E, riboflavin, folacin, iron, and phosphorus. Spinach is high in beta carotene, iron, and calcium.

NUTRITIONAL INFORMATION PER SERVING

Calories	184	Saturated Fat (g)	3
Protein (g)	14	Dietary Fiber (g)	3
Carbohydrate (g)	21	Cholesterol (mg)	83
Fat (g)	6	Sodium (mg)	371
Cal. from Fat (%)	28		

Diabetic Exchanges: 1 lean meat, 0.5 starch, 2 vegetable, 0.5 fat

BREAKFAST CASSEROLE

This egg dish is always a hit and can be prepared ahead of time.
Bringing over uncooked is also an option. Remember, if you prepare
the casserole in a glass dish, place in a cold oven, then turn the
oven on and add 10 to 15 minutes longer to the baking time.

8 slices of white bread, crust removed	1 cup nonfat plain yogurt
3 ounces Canadian bacon, chopped	½ cup grated Parmesan cheese
1 bunch green onions (scallions), chopped	½ teaspoon minced garlic
2 cups broccoli florets	2 tablespoons chopped parsley
5 large eggs, beaten	1 teaspoon dried basil leaves
3 large egg whites	1 tablespoon dried rosemary leaves
2½ cups skim milk	Salt and pepper to taste
1 teaspoon dry mustard	

Arrange the bread along the bottom of a 3-quart oblong casserole
dish or a 13x9x2-inch baking pan, overlapping the slices slightly. In a
small skillet coated with nonstick cooking spray, sauté the bacon, green
onions, and broccoli over medium heat until tender, about 8 minutes.
Spread on top of the bread. In a mixing bowl, blend the eggs, egg
whites, skim milk, and mustard; set aside. In a food processor, blend
the yogurt, Parmesan cheese, garlic, parsley, basil, rosemary, and salt
and pepper. Pour into the egg mixture, stirring until well combined.
Pour over the bread and press the bread down to soak up the liquid.
Cover with plastic wrap and place in the refrigerator for at least
6 hours or overnight. Preheat oven to 375 degrees. Bake for 1 hour, or
until browned and a knife inserted in the center comes out clean.

Makes 12 servings

Doc's Notes:
Bring to a friend the night before so it can be enjoyed freshly baked
the next morning or for a light dinner. Whole wheat bread can be
substituted for the white bread. This dish is high in protein and
contains a cruciferous vegetable.

(see Nutritional Information on next page)

Calories	150	Saturated Fat (g)	2
Protein (g)	12	Dietary Fiber (g)	1
Carbohydrate (g)	15	Cholesterol (mg)	97
Fat (g)	5	Sodium (mg)	358
Cal. from Fat (%)	29		

Diabetic Exchanges: 1 lean meat, 0.5 starch, 0.5 skim milk

CAULIFLOWER SOUP

This smooth soup is so easy to make. Throw all ingredients into a food processor and blend until smooth. Serve hot or cold. When you bring soup, it can be enjoyed any time of day.

4	cups cooked cauliflower flowerets	1⅓ cups buttermilk	
½	cup shredded reduced fat Cheddar cheese	1	cup canned fat-free chicken broth
1	tablespoon all-purpose flour	1	clove garlic, minced
		Salt and pepper to taste	

Place all ingredients in a food processor or blender and process until smooth. Serve immediately or refrigerate if serving cold, heat if soup is to be served hot. Add more broth as needed to thin.

Makes six (1-cup) servings

Doc's Notes:
Cauliflower is a member of the cruciferous vegetable family. Members of this family have been associated with reducing the risk of cancer.

NUTRITIONAL INFORMATION PER SERVING

Calories	76	Saturated Fat (g)	2
Protein (g)	7	Dietary Fiber (g)	2
Carbohydrate (g)	7	Cholesterol (mg)	7
Fat (g)	3	Sodium (mg)	233
Cal. from Fat (%)	29		

Diabetic Exchanges: 0.5 lean meat, 1 vegetable

QUICK AND EASY
CORN AND SHRIMP SOUP

This delicious, easy recipe is a winner. Take to a friend
in plastic containers with the green onions in a separate bag.
They can serve immediately or freeze. I always
double this recipe as it is a family favorite.

1 onion, chopped	2 (14¾-ounce) cans cream-style corn
1 teaspoon minced garlic	
1 green bell pepper, cored and chopped	2 cups skim milk
	1 (10-ounce) can diced tomatoes and green chiles
1 (8-ounce) package fat-free cream cheese, softened	1 pound medium shrimp, peeled
2 (10¾-ounce) cans cream of shrimp soup or corn chowder soup or combination	Sliced green onions, optional

In a heavy large pot, coated with nonstick cooking spray, sauté onion, garlic, and green pepper until tender, about 5 minutes. Stir in cream cheese. Add soup, cream-style corn, milk, tomatoes, and shrimp. Bring to a boil, reduce heat, and cook until shrimp are done, about 10 minutes. Serve with green onions. When reheating soup, if too thick, add more milk.

Makes 8 servings

Doc's Notes:
A cup of this soup will be a great addition to any meal or a complete meal in itself. Low in fat, high in fiber and Vitamin A. Vitamin A helps generate pigment necessary for the proper workings of the retina. It also helps form and maintain healthy skin, teeth, mucous membranes, and skeletal and soft tissue.

NUTRITIONAL INFORMATION PER SERVING

Calories	283	Saturated Fat (g)	2
Protein (g)	20	Dietary Fiber (g)	2
Carbohydrate (g)	41	Cholesterol (mg)	94
Fat (g)	4	Sodium (mg)	1528
Cal. from Fat (%)	16		

Diabetic Exchanges: 1 lean meat, 2 starch, 1 vegetable, 0.5 skim milk

CREAM OF SPINACH SOUP

Frozen broccoli can also be used for a broccoli
soup version. For soup craving, here's an easy idea.
Soups are enjoyed any time of day and freeze well.

½ pound fresh mushrooms, sliced
1 small onion, chopped
2 (10¾-ounce) cans reduced-fat cream of mushroom soup

1¾ cups canned fat-free chicken broth
2 (10-ounce) packages frozen chopped spinach, cooked according to package directions and drained well
Salt and pepper to taste

In a large pot coated with nonstick cooking spray, sauté the mushrooms and onion until tender over medium heat for 5 minutes. Add the soup, chicken broth, spinach, and salt and pepper, stirring until thoroughly heated. Transfer to a food processor or blender to purée.

Makes eight (1-cup) servings

Doc's Notes:

Mushrooms are a good source of B vitamins, copper and other vitamins. Spinach is a good source of vitamins and rich source of beta carotene, protein, and folacin. Folacin is important in the synthesis of DNA, which controls cell function. Folacin acts with B12 to produce red blood cells.

NUTRITIONAL INFORMATION PER SERVING

Calories	76	Saturated Fat (g)	1
Protein (g)	4	Dietary Fiber (g)	3
Carbohydrate (g)	11	Cholesterol (mg)	3
Fat (g)	2	Sodium (mg)	700
Cal. from Fat (%)	24		

Diabetic Exchanges: 0.5 starch, 1 vegetable, 0.5 fat

CHICKEN TORTILLA SOUP

*Popular and a really tasty version of chicken soup. Bring
the condiments over in zip-top bags. Use different flavored tortillas
to make the tortilla strips and make extras to have for snacks.*

Soup

1 onion, chopped
1 teaspoon minced garlic
4 cups canned fat-free
   chicken broth
1 (28-ounce) can diced
   tomatoes

1½ pounds boneless skinless
   chicken breasts, cut into
   chunks
1 tablespoon chili powder
1 teaspoon ground cumin
2 tablespoon lime juice
1 (16-ounce) bag frozen corn

Tortilla Strips and Condiments

6 (8-inch) flour tortillas,
   baked
1 cup shredded reduced-fat
   Cheddar cheese

½ cup sliced green onions
   (scallions)
1 small avocado, peeled and
   diced, optional

In a large pot coated with nonstick cooking spray, sauté the onion and
garlic until tender, about 5 minutes. Add the chicken broth, tomatoes,
chicken, chili powder, cumin, and lime juice and bring mixture to a
boil. Lower heat and continue cooking until chicken is done, about 15
to 20 minutes. Add corn and continue cooking 5 more minutes. Serve
with tortilla strips and condiments.

To make tortilla strips, while soup is cooking, preheat oven to 350
degrees. Cut tortillas into ½-inch wide strips. Coat a baking sheet with
nonstick cooking spray and lay strips over sheet. Bake 15 to 20 minutes
or until lightly browned. Strips may be stored in zip-top bags.

Makes 6 to 8 servings

Doc's Notes:

A dish your whole family will enjoy. Tomatoes are high in lypocene,
and Vitamins A and C. Vitamin C is a member of the antioxidant
family of vitamins. Vitamin C promotes healthy gums and teeth,
aiding in iron absorption and wound healing.

(see Nutritional Information on next page)

Calories	345	Saturated Fat (g)	3
Protein (g)	31	Dietary Fiber (g)	5
Carbohydrate (g)	40	Cholesterol (mg)	57
Fat (g)	7	Sodium (mg)	791
Cal. from Fat (%)	18		

Diabetic Exchanges: 2.5 lean meat, 2 starch, 2 vegetable

RICE TACO SALAD

*Everyone enjoys tacos, so this salad will appeal
to all. It is great even at room temperature.*

1	pound ground sirloin	2	tomatoes, chopped
½	cup finely chopped onion	½	cup shredded reduced-fat
1	clove garlic, minced		Cheddar cheese
½	teaspoon ground cumin	¼	cup nonfat plain yogurt
	Salt and pepper to taste		Picante sauce, optional
3	cups cooked rice		Low-fat tortilla chips, optional
½	head lettuce, shredded		

In a large skillet coated with nonstick cooking spray, cook the beef, onion, and garlic over medium heat, stirring to crumble, about 5 to 7 minutes, or until the meat is done. Drain any excess fat. Add the cumin, salt and pepper, and rice. Remove from the heat and let cool. In a large bowl, combine the lettuce, tomatoes, cheese, and rice mixture. Add the yogurt; toss lightly. Serve immediately with the picante sauce and tortilla chips, if desired.

Makes 6 servings

Doc's Notes:
Try using brown rice for extra fiber.

Calories	289	Saturated Fat (g)	4
Protein (g)	21	Dietary Fiber (g)	2
Carbohydrate (g)	27	Cholesterol (mg)	48
Fat (g)	10	Sodium (mg)	132
Cal. from Fat (%)	32		

Diabetic Exchanges: 2.5 lean meat, 1.5 starch, 1 vegetable

MANICOTTI

*Make in a foil pan so the manicotti can be
frozen or enjoyed that day. Excellent and worth the effort.
Delete the meat for a meatless sauce.*

1 pound ground sirloin
1 large onion, chopped
1 tablespoon minced garlic
3 (15-ounce) cans tomato
  sauce
1 (6-ounce) can tomato paste
1 tablespoon dried basil
  leaves
2 teaspoons dried oregano
  leaves, divided
1 teaspoon sugar
1 tablespoon chopped
  parsley
Salt and pepper to taste

1 (8-ounce) package
  manicotti shells
1 (8-ounce) package fat-free
  cream cheese, softened
1 (16-ounce) carton reduced-
  fat ricotta cheese
2 cups shredded part-skim
  Mozzarella cheese, divided
1 (10-ounce) package frozen
  chopped spinach, thawed
  and squeezed dry
⅓ cup chopped green onion
  (scallions) stems
½ teaspoon black pepper

Preheat oven to 350 degrees. Combine the sirloin, onion, and garlic in a large pot. Cook over medium heat until the meat is done; drain any excess grease. Add the tomato sauce, tomato paste, basil, 1 teaspoon oregano, sugar, parsley, and salt and pepper; bring to a boil. Cover, reduce the heat and simmer 30 minutes to 1 hour (time permitting), stirring occasionally. Meanwhile, cook the manicotti shells according to the package directions, omitting any salt and oil. Drain and let cool. In a large mixing bowl, beat the cream cheese and ricotta cheese until well blended. Stir in 1½ cups mozzarella cheese, spinach, green onion, pepper and remaining 1 teaspoon oregano. Stuff the cream cheese mixture into the cooked shells. Spoon half the sauce mixture into a 3-quart oblong casserole dish coated with nonstick cooking spray. Arrange the stuffed shells over the sauce. Spoon the remaining sauce over the shells. Bake for 30 to 40 minutes or until thoroughly heated. Top with remaining ½ cup mozzarella cheese and bake an additional 5 minutes. Let stand 5 minutes before serving.

Makes 8 servings

Doc's Notes:

Tomatoes provide the Vitamins A and C and spinach is rich in beta carotene and other vitamins and minerals. Beta carotene is a

(continued on next page)

member of the antioxidant family of vitamins. Beta carotene is converted to Vitamin A. Unlike Vitamin A, beta carotene is non-toxic even in large amounts.

NUTRITIONAL INFORMATION PER SERVING

Calories	440	Saturated Fat (g)	6
Protein (g)	35	Dietary Fiber (g)	4
Carbohydrate (g)	44	Cholesterol (mg)	65
Fat (g)	13	Sodium (mg)	1485
Cal. from Fat (%)	28		

Diabetic Exchanges: 3.5 lean meat, 2 starch, 3 vegetable

QUICK CHEESY POTATO SOUP

You would think this rich soup is a no-no, but it's completely painless to make and eat! If you don't like to cook, pay attention to this easy recipe.

1   large onion
2   carrots, peeled
1   green bell pepper, cored
2   (10¾-ounce) cans cream of potato soup
2   cups canned fat-free chicken broth

2   ounces pasteurized processed light cheese spread
1   (8-ounce) carton nonfat plain yogurt

Chop the onion, carrots, and green bell pepper in a food processor. In a large pot coated with nonstick cooking spray, sauté the chopped vegetables over medium heat until tender, about 5 minutes. Add the soup, chicken broth, and cheese, stirring until the cheese is melted and the soup is well heated. Before serving, stir in the yogurt; do not boil.

Makes six (1-cup) servings

NUTRITIONAL INFORMATION PER SERVING

Calories	131	Saturated Fat (g)	1
Protein (g)	7	Dietary Fiber (g)	2
Carbohydrate (g)	20	Cholesterol (mg)	9
Fat (g)	3	Sodium (mg)	1132
Cal. from Fat (%)	21		

Diabetic Exchanges: 0.5 starch, 2 vegetable, 0.5 fat

COMPANY CHICKEN

This fabulous tasting dish and sauce puts it high on any list.
Bring a zip-top bag of wild rice, also. This dish also freezes well.

2 pounds boneless skinless chicken breasts	1 (14-ounce) can artichokes, drained
Salt and pepper to taste	1 cup evaporated skimmed milk
2 tablespoons margarine	
½ pound mushrooms, sliced	½ cup sliced green onion (scallions) stems
½ cup sherry or chicken broth	
2 tablespoons lemon juice	½ cup nonfat plain yogurt

Season the chicken breasts with salt and pepper. In a large skillet coated with nonstick cooking spray, heat the margarine until melted. Brown the chicken on both sides, about 3 to 5 minutes on each side. Add the mushrooms, sherry, and lemon juice. Bring to a boil, reduce the heat and cover, for 20 to 30 minutes or until chicken is done. Add the artichokes and milk, stirring and cooking for 5 more minutes. Stir in the green onion stems and yogurt. Do not boil.

Makes 6 servings

Doc's Notes:
Company Chicken with a salad is a complete meal. High in B Vitamins, copper, and other minerals. B vitamins help convert carbohydrates into energy. A deficiency of B vitamins can cause skin to become dry and cracked.

NUTRITIONAL INFORMATION PER SERVING

Calories	287	Saturated Fat (g)	1
Protein (g)	42	Dietary Fiber (g)	1
Carbohydrate (g)	12	Cholesterol (mg)	90
Fat (g)	6	Sodium (mg)	330
Cal. from Fat (%)	19		

Diabetic Exchanges: 4 lean meat, 0.5 skim milk, 1 vegetable

MEXICAN CHICKEN CASSEROLE

*A layered Mexican casserole that will be appreciated
by all. For a less spicy version, use plain tomatoes.*

1½ cups canned fat-free
    chicken broth
1 cup skim milk
½ cup all-purpose flour
½ cup nonfat plain yogurt
1 (10-ounce) can diced
    tomatoes and green chiles,
    drained
¼ cup chopped parsley
1 tablespoon chili powder
1 teaspoon dried oregano
    leaves

Salt and pepper to taste
1 onion, chopped
1 green bell pepper, cored
    and chopped
2 cloves garlic, minced
10 flour tortillas, cut in quarters
2 cups skinless cooked
    chicken breast chunks
½ cup shredded reduced-fat
    sharp Cheddar cheese

Preheat oven to 350 degrees. In saucepan, bring chicken broth to a simmer. In small bowl, whisk milk into flour to make a smooth paste. Add to chicken broth and cook until thickened and smooth, stirring constantly. Remove from heat and stir in yogurt, tomatoes, parsley, chili powder, and oregano. Season with salt and pepper to taste; set aside. In skillet coated with nonstick cooking spray, sauté onions, green pepper, and garlic until tender. Line bottom of a shallow 3-quart baking dish with half the tortillas. Sprinkle half of the chicken and half of the onion mixture over the tortillas. Spoon half of the sauce evenly on the top. Repeat layers, ending with cheese. Bake for 25 to 30 minutes or until bubbly.

Makes 8 servings

NUTRITIONAL INFORMATION PER SERVING

Calories	268	Saturated Fat (g)	2
Protein (g)	20	Dietary Fiber (g)	3
Carbohydrate (g)	34	Cholesterol (mg)	34
Fat (g)	5	Sodium (mg)	542
Cal. from Fat (%)	18		

Diabetic Exchanges: 2 very lean meat, 2 starch, 1 vegetable

CHICKEN AND BLACK BEAN ENCHILADAS

Adjust the seasoning to your taste for this true Southwestern meal.
Freezes well — freeze before baking and add sauce
when removed from the freezer and ready to bake.

2   pounds skinless, boneless chicken breasts, cut into cubes
Salt and pepper to taste
½   teaspoon minced garlic
1   teaspoon chili powder
1   teaspoon ground cumin
1   (15-ounce) can black beans, drained and rinsed

1   (4-ounce) can chopped green chiles, drained, optional
1   cup sliced green onions (scallions)
1   (8-ounce) package shredded reduced-fat Monterey Jack cheese
24 (8-inch) flour tortillas
Sauce (recipe follows)

Preheat oven to 350 degrees. In a large skillet coated with nonstick cooking spray over a medium-high heat, cook the chicken, stirring occasionally, until done, about 10 minutes. Season with salt and pepper, garlic, chili powder, and cumin. Add the black beans, green chiles, and green onions, stirring to combine. Remove from the heat. Divide the chicken mixture and cheese evenly among the flour tortillas. Roll up each tortilla tightly and place side by side in a 3-quart casserole. Pour the sauce over the enchiladas. Bake, uncovered, for about 30 minutes.

Sauce
½   cup all-purpose flour
1¾ cups canned fat-free chicken broth
2   cups skim milk
½   cup shredded reduced-fat Cheddar cheese

Salt and pepper to taste
1   teaspoon dry mustard
1   tablespoon Worcestershire sauce
1   cup nonfat plain yogurt

In a medium saucepan, place the flour and gradually stir in the chicken broth and milk. Cook, stirring constantly, until the mixture comes to a boil and the sauce thickens. Mix in the cheese, salt and pepper, mustard, and Worcestershire sauce and stir until the cheese melts. Remove from the heat and add the yogurt; do not boil.

Makes 24 enchiladas

Calories	225	Saturated Fat (g)	3
Protein (g)	20	Dietary Fiber (g)	3
Carbohydrate (g)	23	Cholesterol (mg)	29
Fat (g)	6	Sodium (mg)	278
Cal. from Fat (%)	24		

Diabetic Exchanges: 2 lean meat, 1.5 starch

SEAFOOD AND WILD RICE CASSEROLE

An excellent choice! It can be made ahead and reheated.

1	(6-ounce) package long grain and wild rice mix	1	green bell pepper, cored and chopped
1	pound cooked shrimp, peeled	1	onion, chopped
1	pound white crabmeat	½	cup light mayonnaise
1	(10-ounce) package green peas (uncooked)	1	teaspoon Worcestershire sauce
1	cup chopped celery		Salt and pepper to taste

Preheat oven to 350 degrees. Cook rice mix according to directions on package. Combine rice with all remaining ingredients, tossing carefully. Pour into a 2-quart casserole coated with nonstick cooking spray. Bake for 20 to 30 minutes.

Makes 6 to 8 servings

NUTRITIONAL INFORMATION PER SERVING

Calories	287	Saturated Fat (g)	1
Protein (g)	29	Dietary Fiber (g)	3
Carbohydrate (g)	26	Cholesterol (mg)	159
Fat (g)	7	Sodium (mg)	833
Cal. from Fat (%)	21		

Diabetic Exchanges: 4 very lean meat, 1.5 starch, 1 vegetable, 0.5 fat

TURKEY JAMBALAYA

This is a quick and tasty one-dish meal. Jambalaya is a rice mixture combined with seasonings and is a great way to use leftover turkey; you can be a hit twice. Cheat and purchase a roasted chicken to use for the diced turkey.

1 pound turkey sausage or low-fat sausage	1½ pounds cooked, diced turkey breasts or thighs (4 cups)
1 large onion, chopped	
1 pound fresh mushrooms, sliced	1 (14-ounce) can artichoke hearts, quartered
2 (6-ounce) packages long grain and wild rice mix	½ cup chopped green onions (scallions)

Cut sausage into pieces and brown in large pot coated with nonstick cooking spray. Add onions and mushrooms, cooking until tender. Drain off any excess grease. Add wild rice, seasoning packet and water to sausage mixture and cook according to package directions. Add turkey and artichoke hearts, tossing gently. Top with chopped green onions.

Makes 8 to 10 servings

Doc's Notes:

Onions are low in calories, while the mushrooms are rich in B Vitamins and minerals. The artichokes are a great source of Vitamin C and dietary fiber.

NUTRITIONAL INFORMATION PER SERVING

Calories	366	Saturated Fat (g)	3
Protein (g)	36	Dietary Fiber (g)	3
Carbohydrate (g)	35	Cholesterol (mg)	95
Fat (g)	9	Sodium (mg)	979
Cal. from Fat (%)	23		

Diabetic Exchanges: 4 lean meat, 1.5 starch, 2 vegetable

JUMBO STUFFED SHELLS

A simple favorite that I always double when I prepare. Bring over in foil pans to eat immediately or freeze for a later time.

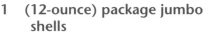

1 (12-ounce) package jumbo shells
1½ pounds ground sirloin
2 large egg whites
¼ cup grated Parmesan cheese
¼ cup bread crumbs
1 tablespoon chopped parsley
1 teaspoon dried basil leaves
½ teaspoon dried oregano leaves
Salt and pepper to taste
1 (29-ounce) jar commercial pasta sauce or tomato sauce
1 (8-ounce) package shredded part skim mozzarella cheese

Preheat oven to 350 degrees. Cook pasta shells according to directions on package omitting oil; drain and set aside. In a skillet, cook sirloin until done. Drain any excess fat. Combine with egg whites, Parmesan cheese, bread crumbs, parsley, basil, oregano, and salt and pepper. Stuff shells with meat filling. Pour half the pasta sauce in a 2-quart baking dish. Arrange stuffed shells on top and cover with remaining sauce. Bake for 20 minutes. Sprinkle with mozzarella cheese and continue baking for 10 minutes longer.

Makes 6 to 8 servings

Doc's Notes:

Everyone seems to enjoy ground beef recipes, and sirloin is a lean cut of beef.

NUTRITIONAL INFORMATION PER SERVING

Calories 478	Saturated Fat (g) 7
Protein (g) 33	Dietary Fiber (g) 3
Carbohydrate (g) 47	Cholesterol (mg) 68
Fat (g) 17	Sodium (mg) 787
Cal. from Fat (%) 32	

Diabetic Exchanges: 3.5 lean meat, 2.5 starch, 2 vegetable, 1 fat

PASTA SALAD

An outstanding pasta salad packed full of great ingredients with a wonderful light dressing.

2 cups snow peas	½ pound fresh mushrooms, cut in half
1 bunch broccoli, flowerets only	1 cup cherry tomatoes, cut in half
1 (12-ounce) package tri-colored pasta shells	1 red bell pepper, cored and cut into strips
1 (6-ounce) package tri-colored stuffed tortellini	⅓ cup grated Romano cheese

Cook snow peas and broccoli in the microwave until crisp tender. Drain and set aside. Cook pasta shells and tortellini according to directions on package omitting salt and oil. Drain and set aside. Combine all ingredients in a large bowl. Toss with Dressing (recipe follows).

Dressing

1 bunch green onions (scallions), sliced	2 teaspoons dried basil leaves
½ cup red wine vinegar	1 teaspoon dried dill weed
⅓ cup olive oil	½ teaspoon dried oregano leaves
2 tablespoons chopped parsley	Salt and pepper to taste
	½ teaspoon sugar
3 cloves garlic, minced	1½ teaspoons Dijon mustard

Combine all ingredients together, mixing well. Pour over pasta salad and refrigerate.

Makes 10 servings

Doc's Notes:

Includes broccoli, a cruciferous vegetable with Vitamins A, B, and C.

NUTRITIONAL INFORMATION PER SERVING

Calories 283	Saturated Fat (g) 2
Protein (g) 10	Dietary Fiber (g) 4
Carbohydrate (g) 40	Cholesterol (mg) 13
Fat (g) 10	Sodium (mg) 334
Cal. from Fat (%) 31	

Diabetic Exchanges: 2 starch, 2 vegetable, 1.5 fat

SHRIMP-RICE CASSEROLE

The hint of cheese and salsa makes this an outstanding quick shrimp and rice dish. Adjust the seasoning to how well you can tolerate them.

1   onion, chopped
1   teaspoon minced garlic
½   cup chopped red or green bell pepper
1½ pounds medium shrimp, peeled
1   (8-ounce) can mushroom stems and pieces, drained
1½ cups shredded reduced-fat Cheddar cheese
⅓   cup salsa

1   tablespoon Worcestershire sauce
½   cup evaporated skimmed milk
1   bunch green onions (scallions), sliced, optional
2   tablespoons canned diced green chiles, drained, optional
3   cups cooked white or brown rice

In a large skillet coated with nonstick cooking spray, sauté the onion, garlic, pepper, shrimp, and mushrooms over medium-high heat for about 5 to 7 minutes. Add the cheese, salsa, Worcestershire sauce, evaporated milk, green onions, and green chiles. Stir in the rice and cook until the cheese is melted and well combined.

Makes 6 servings

Doc's Notes:

Buy peeled shrimp or have a friend peel them for you. You do not want to prick your finger on a shrimp shell while your white blood cell count is low. Wonderful dish!

NUTRITIONAL INFORMATION PER SERVING

Calories	317	Saturated Fat (g)	4
Protein (g)	31	Dietary Fiber (g)	2
Carbohydrate (g)	31	Cholesterol (mg)	177
Fat (g)	6	Sodium (mg)	648
Cal. from Fat (%)	18		

Diabetic Exchanges: 3.5 very lean meat, 1.5 starch, 1 vegetable

PRETZEL STRAWBERRY GELATIN

This delicious recipe will even pass for dessert. A great choice!

4 tablespoons margarine, melted

2 tablespoons light brown sugar

2 cups crushed pretzels

1 (6-ounce) package strawberry gelatin

2 cups boiling water

3 cups sliced fresh strawberries

4 ounces fat-free cream cheese

½ cup sugar

1 (1.3-ounce) envelope dry whipped topping mix

½ cup skim milk

Preheat oven to 350 degrees. Combine margarine, brown sugar and pretzels and press into a 13x9x2-inch baking pan. Bake for 10 minutes; cool. Meanwhile dissolve strawberry gelatin in boiling water, stirring until dissolved. Add sliced strawberries. Cool in refrigerator until gelatin begins to set. In mixer, beat cream cheese with sugar. Prepare whipped topping according to directions on package substituting skim milk. Fold into cream cheese mixture. Spread over cooled crust. Pour semi-firm gelatin mixture over cream cheese layer. Refrigerate until congealed.

Makes 16 servings

Doc's Notes:

Gelatin is great for your nails which are sometimes weakened by chemotherapy. This is also a great source of Vitamin C and potassium.

NUTRITIONAL INFORMATION PER SERVING

Calories	163	Saturated Fat (g)	1
Protein (g)	3	Dietary Fiber (g)	1
Carbohydrate (g)	30	Cholesterol (mg)	1
Fat (g)	4	Sodium (mg)	258
Cal. from Fat (%)	20		

Diabetic Exchanges: 0.5 starch, 1.5 other carb., 0.5 fat

CHOCOLATE LAYERED DESSERT

Easy, a favorite, and will satisfy that
sweet tooth when you want dessert.

Crust

1 cup flour	½ cup chopped pecans
7 tablespoons margarine	

Preheat oven to 350 degrees. Mix all ingredients and press into an ungreased 13x9x2-inch pan. Bake for 20 minutes. Cool and then top with Cream Cheese Layer (recipe follows).

Cream Cheese Layer

¾ cup frozen fat-free
  whipped topping

1 (8-ounce) package fat-free
  cream cheese
⅔ cup powdered sugar

Combine ingredients in mixer and beat only until well blended. Spread on top of first layer. Top with Pudding Layer (recipe follows).

Pudding Layer

1 (4-serving) package instant
  vanilla pudding
1 (4-serving) package instant
  chocolate pudding

3 cups skim milk
1 teaspoon vanilla extract
1¼ cups frozen fat-free
  whipped topping, thawed

Mix pudding with milk and beat according to directions on package. After thickened, add vanilla. Spread on top of Cream Cheese Layer. Cover dessert with whipped topping.

Makes 16 servings

Doc's Notes:

It is hard to believe this is low fat. Vanilla nutritional energy drink supplement can be substituted for the skim milk to turn this into a high calorie dessert. This is an easily tolerated choice.

NUTRITIONAL INFORMATION PER SERVING

Calories 207	Saturated Fat (g) 1
Protein (g) 5	Dietary Fiber (g) 1
Carbohydrate (g) 29	Cholesterol (mg) 2
Fat (g) 8	Sodium (mg) 333
Cal. from Fat (%) 34	

Diabetic Exchanges: 0.5 starch, 1.5 other carb., 1.5 fat

SWEET POTATO POUND CAKE

*The orange glaze over the spicy moist cake will make
this a sensational choice for dessert. Sweet potatoes
are rich in beta carotene, and Vitamins C and E.*

½ cup margarine
1 cup sugar
1 large egg
3 large egg whites
2 (15-ounce) cans sweet
  potatoes (yams), drained
  and mashed (about 2
  cups)
1 teaspoon vanilla extract
2½ cups all-purpose flour
1 teaspoon baking powder

1 teaspoon baking soda
1 teaspoon ground cinnamon
½ teaspoon ground nutmeg
1 teaspoon grated orange
  rind
⅓ cup flaked coconut
½ cup coarsely chopped
  walnuts, optional
2-3 tablespoons orange juice
1 cup confectioners' sugar

Preheat oven to 350 degrees. In a mixing bowl, beat together margarine and sugar until blended. Add egg and egg whites, one at a time, beating well after each addition. Mix in sweet potatoes and vanilla. In another bowl, mix together flour, baking powder, baking soda, cinnamon, nutmeg, and orange rind. Gradually spoon flour mixture into creamed mixture, beating well after each addition. Stir in coconut and walnuts. Pour batter into a 10-inch Bundt pan coated with nonstick cooking spray. Bake 45 to 50 minutes or until a wooden pick inserted in center of cake comes out clean. Cool in pan for 10 minutes; invert onto a serving plate. In a small bowl, mix together orange juice and confectioners' sugar to make a glaze. Spoon glaze over cake.

Makes 16 servings

NUTRITIONAL INFORMATION PER SERVING

Calories 249
Protein (g) 4
Carbohydrate (g) 44
Fat (g) 7
Cal. from Fat (%) 24

Saturated Fat (g) 2
Dietary Fiber (g) 1
Cholesterol (mg) 13
Sodium (mg) 219

Diabetic Exchanges: 1.5 starch, 1.5 other carb., 1 fat

PIÑA COLADA BUNDT CAKE

Begin with a mix to end with a fabulous cake.
Easy to travel with this cake.

1   (18¼-ounce) box reduced-fat yellow cake mix
1   (4-serving) package instant vanilla pudding and pie filling
1½ cups piña colada drink mix, divided
⅓   cup canola oil
2   large eggs
2   large egg whites
⅓   cup flaked coconut
1   (8-ounce) can crushed pineapple, in its own juice, undrained
1   cup confectioner's sugar

Preheat oven to 350 degrees. In a mixing bowl, blend together the cake mix, pudding, 1 cup piña colada mix, oil, eggs, and egg whites until creamy, about 2 minutes. Stir in the coconut and pineapple, mixing well. Pour the batter into a 10-inch Bundt pan coated with nonstick cooking spray and dusted with flour. Bake for 45 minutes or until toothpick inserted comes out clean. Cool in pan 10 minutes and then invert onto a serving platter. Poke holes in top of cake with a toothpick. In a small bowl, combine the remaining ½ cup piña colada mix and confectioner's sugar, mixing well. Slowly drizzle over the cake.

Makes 16 servings

NUTRITIONAL INFORMATION PER SERVING

Calories	263	Saturated Fat (g)	2
Protein (g)	3	Dietary Fiber (g)	0
Carbohydrate (g)	49	Cholesterol (mg)	27
Fat (g)	7	Sodium (mg)	321
Cal. from Fat (%)	23		

Diabetic Exchanges: 1 starch, 2 other carb., 1 fat

SWEET POTATO CHEESECAKE

Yams add nutrition to America's favorite dessert.
For a short cut, purchase a commercially prepared reduced-fat
9-inch graham cracker crust and fill with cheesecake batter.

1   cup graham cracker crumbs
2   tablespoons sugar
½   teaspoon ground cinnamon
¼   teaspoon ground allspice
2   tablespoons margarine,
      melted
2   (8-ounce) packages light
      cream cheese
1   cup nonfat plain yogurt

1   (15-ounce) can sweet
      potatoes (yams), drained
      and mashed, or 1 cup
      fresh cooked and mashed
1⅓ cups dark brown sugar
1   large egg
1   large egg white
2   teaspoons vanilla extract

In a bowl, combine the cracker crumbs, sugar, cinnamon, allspice, and margarine. Pat into the bottom and up the sides of a 9-inch springform pan. In a large bowl, beat together cream cheese and yogurt until creamy. Add yams and brown sugar, beating until smooth. Add egg and egg white one at a time, beating after each addition. Add vanilla. Spoon mixture into crust. Bake 50 to 60 minutes or until set. Remove from oven to cool. Refrigerate until chilled, about 2 hours.

Makes 10 to 12 servings

Doc's Notes:
Sweet potatoes are rich in beta carotene, Vitamin C and Vitamin E.

NUTRITIONAL INFORMATION PER SERVING

Calories	285	Saturated Fat (g)	5
Protein (g)	7	Dietary Fiber (g)	1
Carbohydrate (g)	43	Cholesterol (mg)	36
Fat (g)	9	Sodium (mg)	311
Cal. from Fat (%)	30		

Diabetic Exchanges: 1 starch, 2 other carb., 2 fat

HEALTHY EATING POST TREATMENT

❖ *Do I have to follow a special diet?*

❖ *Is it okay to eat raw fruits and vegetables?*

❖ *Are there any foods that decrease my risk of cancer?*

❖ *What is the most important food to decrease for healthy living —
you're right — **FAT!***

❖ *What about carcinogens — a cancer producing substance?*

Once your treatments are over, you will hopefully start to feel better and are eager to try new foods. Your taste buds are alert and again ready to be stimulated. You do not have to worry about your blood count being low or your mouth being sore. Hopefully, your bowel habits have normalized. It is fine to eat raw fruits and vegetables.

Salt-cured and pickled foods contain natural carcinogens that may increase your risk of developing stomach and esophageal cancers. Nitrates and nitrites, used to preserve meats, can enhance the formation of nitrosoamine, another carcinogen. Smoked foods can absorb carcinogens out of the smoke.

The good foods, such as whole grains, legumes, fruits, and vegetables, will decrease your risk of cancer. These foods all contain dietary fiber, which is thought to protect against colon cancer. Diets high in fruits and vegetables are believed to protect against bladder, prostate, stomach, esophageal, and lung cancer. Please do not forget smoking is the very worst carcinogen around. Smoking is responsible for lung, bladder, esophageal, and head and neck cancer. Eat healthy, but PLEASE DO NOT SMOKE. Cruciferous vegetables (kale, cauliflower, broccoli) may also reduce your risk of cancer. Foods rich in vitamin C can protect against cancers of the mouth, esophagus, pancreas, and stomach.

Vitamins A and E may help protect against certain cancers by acting as antioxidants, and in the case of vitamin E, by inhibiting the conversion of nitrites into nitrosamines. Green tea may protect against some cancers by stimulating the activity of antioxidant and detoxifying enzymes.

Also note that a diet that reduces your risk of developing cancer can also reduce your risk of developing heart disease. It can also decrease your risk of developing diverticulitis and irritable bowel syndrome, both of which have been linked to a diet low in fiber.

There are more studies on fat than on any dietary risk factor. There is good evidence that fat increases your risk of developing cancer, especially cancer of the prostate, colon, breast, ovary, endometrium, and pancreas. The National Cancer Institute (NCI) and the American Cancer Society both recommend that you limit your fat intake to 30% or less of the calories you consume.

How can you cut down on fat:

(1) Eat skinless chicken breasts.

(2) Buy extra-lean ground beef as in sirloin.

(3) Replace meat with beans or fish.

(4) Replace whole milk with nonfat or 1% milk.

(5) Replace ice cream with sherbet or frozen yogurt.

(6) Substitute croissants and breakfast bars with bagels, English muffins, pita bread or corn tortillas.

(7) Be conscious of your choice of food.

Remember you do not have to deprive yourself forever of the foods you love. If you overdo it one day, make allowances the next day or two. The method of healthy eating Monday through Friday and splurging on the weekends sometimes works well for people. It is important that you find the balance of what works best for you. Your goal is a long term healthy lifestyle. With all these tasty recipes, you will find that your diet will not be different than the next person as it is the approach in preparation of these recipes that has changed. Enjoy eating and staying healthy.

Dietary Suggestions for A Healthy Diet

- Keep your total fat intake at or below 30% of your total calories, and limit your intake of saturated fats—which contribute to high blood cholesterol levels—to no more than 10% of your total calories.

- Limit your intake of dietary cholesterol to no more than 300 milligrams per day.

- Get at least 55% of your total daily calories from carbohydrates, preferably complex carbohydrates—the starches in grains, legumes, vegetables, and some fruits. These foods can also provide you with the 20 to 30 grams of dietary fiber that is recommended daily, as well as vitamins and minerals.

- Protein should make up only about 12 to 15% of your daily calories - the protein should come from low-fat sources.

- ✦ Avoid too much sugar; it contributes to tooth decay, and many foods high in sugar are also high in fat.
- ✦ Try to limit your sodium to no more than 2400 milligrams per day, the equivalent of a little more than a teaspoon of salt.
- ✦ Maintain an adequate intake of vitamins and minerals—particularly of iron and calcium.
- ✦ If you drink alcohol, do so in moderation—no more than one ounce of alcohol a day, if at all.

Guidelines To Prevent Cancer

- ✦ Reduce saturated fat intake.
- ✦ Increase consumption of fruits and vegetables, especially cruciferous.
- ✦ Reduce consumption of salt-cured and smoked foods.
- ✦ Continue efforts to minimize contamination of foods with carcinogens from any source.
- ✦ Consume alcohol in moderation, if at all.

OATMEAL PANCAKES

These hearty whole grain pancakes are wonderful. Try cutting up bananas in the batter or top with sliced fruit instead of syrup.

½ cup whole wheat flour	1½ cups cooked oatmeal
1 teaspoon baking powder	¾ cup skim milk
1 tablespoon light brown sugar	1 tablespoon canola oil
½ teaspoon ground cinnamon	1 large egg

Mix together flour, baking powder, sugar, and cinnamon. Stir into oatmeal. Mix milk, oil, and egg together and add to batter. Cook pancakes on a heated skillet coated with nonstick cooking spray.

Makes about 10 pancakes

Doc's Notes:
A great way to include fiber in your meal. Top with blueberries for a big dose of antioxidants.

NUTRITIONAL INFORMATION PER SERVING

Calories	74	Saturated Fat (g)	0
Protein (g)	3	Dietary Fiber (g)	1
Carbohydrate (g)	11	Cholesterol (mg)	22
Fat (g)	2	Sodium (mg)	66
Cal. from Fat (%)	28		

Diabetic Exchanges: 0.5 starch, 0.5 fat

MANGO SALAD

The sauce keeps in refrigerator a long time.
If you have extra sauce, serve over frozen yogurt.

3　(3-ounce) packages lemon
　　gelatin
3　cups boiling water

1　(32-ounce) jar mangos with
　　juice
1　(8-ounce) package light
　　cream cheese

Dissolve gelatin in boiling water. Place mangos with juice in a food processor. Gradually add cream cheese and blend well. Stir in gelatin mixture. Pour into a 2-quart mold coated with nonstick cooking spray. Refrigerate until set. Serve with Sauce (recipe follows).

Sauce

1　egg, slightly beaten
⅔　cup sugar

Juice of 1 lemon
Juice of 1 orange

Place all ingredients in small saucepan and bring to boil; boil 5 to 7 minutes. Remove from heat and cool. Store sauce in refrigerator. Take out 30 minutes before serving to soften.

Makes 12 servings

Doc's Notes:
Light and healthy and a great source of beta carotene and Vitamins C and E.

NUTRITIONAL INFORMATION PER SERVING

Calories	154	Saturated Fat (g)	2
Protein (g)	3	Dietary Fiber (g)	1
Carbohydrate (g)	28	Cholesterol (mg)	27
Fat (g)	4	Sodium (mg)	125
Cal. from Fat (%)	20		

Diabetic Exchanges: 0.5 fruit, 1.5 other carb., 1 fat

CREAM OF SPINACH AND BRIE SOUP

Sneak spinach into your diet with this wonderful creamy soup. Try using Swiss chard for spinach to include a cruciferous vegetable. This is a little high in saturated fat but perfect to entice your appetite. I couldn't leave this recipe out.

½   cup chopped onion
⅓   cup all-purpose flour
2   cups skim milk
2   cups canned fat-free chicken broth

8   ounces brie cheese, rind removed and cubed
2   cups fresh spinach, washed and stemmed
Salt and pepper to taste

In a nonstick pot coated with nonstick cooking spray, sauté onion until soft. Stir in flour. Gradually stir in milk and chicken broth. Bring to a boil over medium heat, stirring constantly, until thickened. Add cheese and stir until melted. Add spinach and salt and pepper, stirring until spinach is wilted.

Makes 6 servings

Doc's Notes:
Spinach is a great source of iron, Vitamin A, and calcium. Iron is essential to the formation of hemoglobin, which carries oxygen in the blood, and myoglobin, which carries oxygen in muscle.

NUTRITIONAL INFORMATION PER SERVING

Calories 192	Saturated Fat (g) 7
Protein (g) 13	Dietary Fiber (g) 1
Carbohydrate (g) 11	Cholesterol (mg) 39
Fat (g) 11	Sodium (mg) 495
Cal. from Fat (%) 50	

Diabetic Exchanges: 1 high fat meat, 0.5 starch, 0.5 skim milk

BEEFY VEGETABLE SOUP

This makes a huge pot of soup. Freeze in containers and have dinner in only minutes. Remember, you can always add your favorite fresh or frozen vegetables to the pot. Great way to clean out the refrigerator. For a quick version, use cans of beef broth.

2 pounds extra-lean stewing beef, cubed	1 (16-ounce) package frozen cut green beans
1 pound cross-cut beef shank, cubed	1 (16-ounce) package baby carrots
6 quarts water	2 cups shredded cabbage
Salt and pepper to taste	2 (28-ounce) cans no-salt added whole tomatoes, with their juice
1 large onion, chopped	
1 cup chopped celery	
1 (16-ounce) package frozen corn	2 bay leaves
	1 (8-ounce) package small shell pasta

In a very large pot, place the stewing beef, beef shank, and 6 quarts of water. Season with salt and pepper. Bring to a boil and boil 1 to 1½ hours over medium heat. Add the onion, celery, corn, green beans, carrots, cabbage, tomatoes, and bay leaves. Continue cooking for 1 hour. Add the pasta and cook until the pasta is done and meat is tender, about 10 to 15 minutes. Season to taste and remove the bay leaves before serving. Add more water or beef broth if soup gets too thick.

Makes sixteen (1-cup) servings

Doc's Notes:
High fiber content with a great source of Vitamin A and C. Cabbage is a cruciferous vegetable.

NUTRITIONAL INFORMATION PER SERVING

Calories	237	Saturated Fat (g)	1
Protein (g)	24	Dietary Fiber (g)	4
Carbohydrate (g)	27	Cholesterol (mg)	46
Fat (g)	4	Sodium (mg)	75
Cal. from Fat (%)	15		

Diabetic Exchanges: 2.5 very lean meat, 1 starch, 3 vegetable

Healthy Eating Post Treatment

COUSCOUS SALAD

*Couscous only takes minutes to prepare and this
wonderful combination of cranberries, snow peas,
and peanuts makes this recipe a wonderful choice.*

1 teaspoon minced garlic, divided	1 (10-ounce) package snow peas, cooked crisp tender according to directions
4 tablespoons lemon juice, divided	5 green onions (scallions), sliced
2½ cups canned fat-free chicken broth	½ cup peanuts
1½ cups couscous	½ cup dried cranberries
⅓ cup chopped fresh parsley	2 tablespoons olive oil
	Dash of hot pepper sauce

In a pot coated with nonstick cooking spray, sauté ½ teaspoon garlic
and add 1 tablespoon lemon juice and chicken broth. Bring to a full
boil and add couscous, cover pot and remove from heat. Let sit for 5
minutes, fluff with a fork and add parsley. Set aside to cool. When
cool, add snow peas, green onions, peanuts, and cranberries. For dressing, mix together remaining ½ teaspoon minced garlic and 3 tablespoons lemon juice, oil, and hot sauce. Toss the dressing with the
couscous mixture.

Makes 8 to 10 servings

NUTRITIONAL INFORMATION PER SERVING

Calories	204	Saturated Fat (g)	1
Protein (g)	7	Dietary Fiber (g)	4
Carbohydrate (g)	30	Cholesterol (mg)	0
Fat (g)	7	Sodium (mg)	162
Cal. from Fat (%)	29		

Diabetic Exchanges: 1.5 starch, 0.5 fruit, 1 fat

PAELLA SALAD

This attractive salad of many colors and textures will convince even the heartiest eaters that a salad can make a satisfying meal. The shrimp may be left out.

2   (5-ounce) packages saffron yellow rice
¼   cup balsamic vinegar
¼   cup lemon juice
1   tablespoon olive oil
1   teaspoon dried basil leaves
⅛   teaspoon black pepper
Dash of cayenne pepper
1   pound medium shrimp, peeled and cooked
1   (14-ounce) can quartered artichoke hearts, drained

¾   cup chopped green bell pepper
1   cup frozen green peas, thawed
1   cup chopped tomato
1   (2-ounce) jar diced pimentos, drained
½   cup chopped red onion
2   ounces chopped prosciutto, optional

Prepare the rice according to package directions, omitting any oil and salt. Set aside. In a small bowl, mix together the vinegar, lemon juice, oil, basil, black pepper, and cayenne pepper; set dressing aside. In a large bowl, combine the cooked rice with the shrimp, artichoke hearts, green pepper, peas, tomato, pimentos, red onion, and prosciutto, mixing well. Pour the dressing over the rice mixture, tossing to coat. Cover and refrigerate at least 2 hours before serving.

Makes 6 servings

Doc's Notes:
Low in fat and high in fiber.

NUTRITIONAL INFORMATION PER SERVING

Calories 290	Saturated Fat (g) 1
Protein (g) 17	Dietary Fiber (g) 3
Carbohydrate (g) 50	Cholesterol (mg) 90
Fat (g) 3	Sodium (mg) 871
Cal. from Fat (%) 9	

Diabetic Exchanges: 1.5 very lean meat, 3 starch, 1 vegetable

SEVEN-LAYER SALAD

A fantastic make-ahead layered salad with a divine dressing.

½ cup nonfat plain yogurt
½ cup buttermilk
½ cup crumbled feta cheese
  (about 2 ounces)
1 teaspoon sugar
¼ teaspoon dried dill weed
½ teaspoon dried basil leaves
⅛ teaspoon ground white
  pepper
1 (9-ounce) package spinach
  tortellini

6 cups torn fresh spinach
  leaves
½ pound fresh mushrooms,
  sliced
2 Roma (plum) tomatoes,
  chopped
4 green onions (scallions),
  chopped
2½ ounces sliced Canadian
  bacon, pan-cooked and
  cut into pieces, optional

In a food processor, blend the yogurt, buttermilk, feta cheese, sugar, dill weed, basil, and pepper until smooth to make a dressing. Chill. Cook the tortellini according to package directions, omitting any oil and salt. Drain and rinse in cold water. In a 3-quart oblong dish, layer the spinach leaves, tortellini, mushrooms, tomatoes, and green onions. Pour the dressing over the salad and sprinkle with the bacon. Cover and refrigerate at least 2 hours or overnight to blend the flavors until serving time.

Makes 8 to 10 servings

Doc's Notes:
Spinach is high in iron, Vitamin A and calcium. The tomatoes provide Vitamins A and C.

NUTRITIONAL INFORMATION PER SERVING

Calories	96	Saturated Fat (g)	2
Protein (g)	6	Dietary Fiber (g)	1
Carbohydrate (g)	10	Cholesterol (mg)	40
Fat (g)	4	Sodium (mg)	176
Cal. from Fat (%)	35		

Diabetic Exchanges: 1 lean meat, 0.5 starch

SWEET AND SOUR BROCCOLI SALAD

This salad will receive rave reviews.

4 cups broccoli florets, cut in small pieces
½ cup sliced green onions (scallions)
2 cups red or green grapes, or combination
1 head red tip lettuce, torn into pieces
1 tablespoon margarine
¼ cup slivered almonds
½ cup red wine vinegar
¼ cup sugar
2 tablespoons reduced-sodium soy sauce
1 tablespoon olive oil

In a large bowl, combine the broccoli, green onions, grapes, and lettuce; set aside. In a small skillet coated with nonstick cooking spray, melt the margarine. Add the almonds and sauté until light brown; set aside. In a small bowl, whisk together the red wine vinegar, sugar, soy sauce, and olive oil. Pour over the broccoli mixture and toss. Stir in the browned almonds.

Makes 6 servings

Doc's Notes:
Broccoli is in the cruciferous family. Broccoli contains indoles which are effective in protecting against certain forms of cancer. It has a rich supply of vitamins and minerals.

NUTRITIONAL INFORMATION PER SERVING

Calories	165	Saturated Fat (g)	1
Protein (g)	4	Dietary Fiber (g)	3
Carbohydrate (g)	23	Cholesterol (mg)	0
Fat (g)	8	Sodium (mg)	242
Cal. from Fat (%)	39		

Diabetic Exchanges: 0.5 fruit, 1 vegetable, 0.5 other carb., 1.5 fat

CAESAR SALAD

You will not miss the "real thing" with this duplication.
For a light dinner, top with grilled chicken.

2	tablespoons grated Parmesan cheese	1	tablespoon olive oil
2	tablespoons water	1	clove garlic
2	tablespoons red wine vinegar	¼	teaspoon dry mustard
1	teaspoon Worcestershire sauce	1	large bunch romaine lettuce, cleaned and torn into pieces
		⅓	cup croutons, optional

Combine all ingredients except lettuce and croutons in a food processor and blend until smooth. Pour over lettuce, tossing well. Top with croutons, if desired.

Makes 4 servings

Doc's Notes:
Romaine lettuce is a little more nutritious than iceberg. Great source of Vitamin A, beta carotene, Vitamin C, and folacin.

NUTRITIONAL INFORMATION PER SERVING

Calories	63	Saturated Fat (g)	1
Protein (g)	3	Dietary Fiber (g)	2
Carbohydrate (g)	3	Cholesterol (mg)	3
Fat (g)	5	Sodium (mg)	82
Cal. from Fat (%)	61		

Diabetic Exchanges: 1 vegetable, 1 fat

RASPBERRY SPINACH SALAD

This salad is truly outstanding.
Toss with toasted pine nuts for that extra special touch.
For a change, use a variety of lettuce instead of spinach.

3 tablespoons raspberry vinegar
3 tablespoons seedless raspberry jam
¼ cup canola oil

8 cups fresh spinach, rinsed, stemmed, and torn into pieces
1 cup fresh raspberries or sliced strawberries
3 kiwis, peeled and sliced

Combine vinegar and jam in a food processor or blender. With processor running, add oil in a thin stream, blending well. In a large bowl, carefully toss spinach, raspberries, and kiwis with dressing. Serve immediately.

Makes 8 servings

Doc's Notes:
Get in the habit of adding fruit of your choice to your salad.

NUTRITIONAL INFORMATION PER SERVING

Calories	115	Saturated Fat (g)	1
Protein (g)	1	Dietary Fiber (g)	3
Carbohydrate (g)	13	Cholesterol (mg)	0
Fat (g)	7	Sodium (mg)	26
Cal. from Fat (%)	53		

Diabetic Exchanges: 0.5 fruit, 0.5 other carb., 1.5 fat

TROPICAL GREEN SALAD

Depending on the time of year, use available fruit instead of nectarines to create this tropical paradise salad. Avocado and olive oil are great choices for monounsaturated fat, which has been cited as preventative for cancer.

2	cups sugar snap peas	¼	cup sunflower seeds
6	cups torn assorted lettuce	½	cup thinly sliced red onion
1	avocado, pitted and cut into 1-inch cubes	¼	cup lime juice
		2	tablespoons olive oil
3	nectarines, sliced	3	tablespoons honey

Cook the sugar snap peas in a covered microwave dish in a small amount of water, about 4 minutes or until crisp tender. Drain, rinse with cold water, and set aside. In a large bowl, combine the cooked snap peas, lettuce, avocado, nectarines, sunflower seeds, and onion. In a small bowl, whisk together the lime juice, oil, and honey. Toss dressing with salad mixture.

Makes 8 servings

NUTRITIONAL INFORMATION PER SERVING

Calories	165	Saturated Fat (g)	1
Protein (g)	3	Dietary Fiber (g)	5
Carbohydrate (g)	20	Cholesterol (mg)	0
Fat (g)	9	Sodium (mg)	11
Cal. from Fat (%)	47		

Diabetic Exchanges: 0.5 fruit, 1 vegetable, 0.5 other carb., 2 fat

SPINACH RICE WITH FETA

Adjust the onion and mushrooms to your preferences.
Spinach and feta compliment each other, however,
the cheese of choice can be used or even delete cheese.

1 cup dry brown rice	1 tablespoon lemon juice
2¼ cups canned fat-free chicken broth	1 teaspoon dried oregano leaves
1 medium onion, chopped	1 (10-ounce) bag fresh
½ pound sliced mushrooms	spinach leaves, stemmed
½ teaspoon minced garlic	½ cup crumbled feta cheese

In a saucepan, combine rice and broth. Bring to a boil, stir, and reduce heat. Cover and simmer for 45 minutes or until rice is tender. Meanwhile, in a large skillet coated with nonstick cooking spray, sauté the onion, mushrooms, and garlic until tender. Stir in lemon juice and oregano. Add spinach, cooking only until wilted. Toss cooked rice with spinach mixture. Sprinkle with cheese and serve.

Makes 6 servings

Doc's Notes:
Spinach is a wonderful source of minerals.

NUTRITIONAL INFORMATION PER SERVING

Calories	184	Saturated Fat (g)	2
Protein (g)	8	Dietary Fiber (g)	3
Carbohydrate (g)	31	Cholesterol (mg)	11
Fat (g)	4	Sodium (mg)	414
Cal. from Fat (%)	18		

Diabetic Exchanges: 1.5 starch, 1 vegetable, 0.5 fat

FRIED RICE STIR-FRY

Turn that leftover rice into a light veggie meal. The eggs give the dish protein. If you have sesame oil, you may add a tablespoon instead of the last tablespoon peanut oil.

2 large eggs	4 cups cooked white or brown rice
2 tablespoons peanut oil, divided	1 bunch green onions (scallions), sliced
1 onion, chopped	
1 tablespoon minced garlic	⅓ cup sliced water chestnuts
¼ cup reduced sodium soy sauce	1 cup frozen green peas

Coat a 12-inch nonstick skillet with nonstick cooking spray and set it over medium heat. Beat the eggs lightly, pour them into the skillet, and cook without stirring until they are almost dry. When the eggs are ready, remove them to a plate and cut into strips; set aside. In the same skillet, heat 1 tablespoon oil and sauté the onion and garlic until tender. Add the soy sauce, rice, and remaining 1 tablespoon oil, stirring until well heated. Add the green onions, water chestnuts, and peas, stir frying until well heated. Gently mix in the egg strips and serve.

Makes 6 servings

NUTRITIONAL INFORMATION PER SERVING

Calories	247	Saturated Fat (g)	1
Protein (g)	8	Dietary Fiber (g)	3
Carbohydrate (g)	39	Cholesterol (mg)	71
Fat (g)	7	Sodium (mg)	453
Cal. from Fat (%)	24		

Diabetic Exchanges: 2 starch, 2 vegetable, 1 fat

CURRIED RICE AND SWEET POTATOES

If you enjoy curry, this team of rice and sweet potatoes makes a great side dish. By including apples, raisins, and peas you have a variety of nutrients in one dish.

½ cup chopped onion
½ teaspoon minced garlic
1 cup dry rice
2 cups water
2 cups peeled and diced
  sweet potatoes (yams)

1 cup peeled and chopped
  Granny Smith apple
1 cup frozen peas
⅓ cup golden raisins
½ cup walnuts, toasted
1 teaspoon curry powder
Salt to taste

In a pot coated with nonstick cooking spray, sauté the onion and garlic until tender. Add the rice, water, and sweet potatoes; bring to a boil. Cover, reduce heat, and simmer 15 minutes or until the liquid is absorbed. Carefully stir in the apple, peas, raisins, walnuts, curry, and salt.

Makes 6 servings

NUTRITIONAL INFORMATION PER SERVING

Calories 277
Protein (g) 6
Carbohydrate (g) 51
Fat (g) 6
Cal. from Fat (%) 19

Saturated Fat (g) 1
Dietary Fiber (g) 5
Cholesterol (mg) 0
Sodium (mg) 36

Diabetic Exchanges: 2.5 starch, 1 fruit, 1 fat

EASY BROCCOLI POTATO BAKE

By including broccoli in this easy, fabulous potato dish,
you are getting in your veggies. The broccoli
can be omitted for a plain potato bake.

2 (10-ounce) packages
 frozen broccoli, thawed
1 (32-ounce) bag frozen
 hash brown potatoes
2 cups shredded reduced-fat
 sharp Cheddar cheese

1 (16-ounce) container low-
 fat cottage cheese
2 cups nonfat plain yogurt
Salt and pepper to taste
Paprika

Preheat oven to 350 degrees. In a 3-quart casserole dish coated with nonstick cooking spray, combine all ingredients except paprika, mixing well. Sprinkle with paprika. Bake 1 hour 15 minutes to 1 hour 30 minutes or until casserole is bubbly.

Makes 8 to 10 servings

Doc's Notes:
Another way to get cruciferous vegetables in your diet.

NUTRITIONAL INFORMATION PER SERVING

Calories	214	Saturated Fat (g)	3
Protein (g)	18	Dietary Fiber (g)	3
Carbohydrate (g)	25	Cholesterol (mg)	19
Fat (g)	5	Sodium (mg)	361
Cal. from Fat (%)	22		

Diabetic Exchanges: 1.5 lean meat, 1 starch, 0.5 skim milk, 1 vegetable

CAULIFLOWER SUPREME

Purchase cauliflower and broccoli flowerets for an easy combo.

1 head cauliflower, cut into flowerets
⅓ cup water
½ cup nonfat plain yogurt

½ cup shredded reduced fat sharp Cheddar cheese
½ teaspoon dry mustard
Dash of cayenne pepper
Salt and pepper to taste

Preheat oven to 400 degrees. Cook cauliflower in ⅓ cup water, covered, in microwave for 8 minutes or until crisp tender. Drain and transfer to a baking dish coated with nonstick cooking spray. Combine yogurt with remaining ingredients and spread over cauliflower. Bake, uncovered, for 8 to 10 minutes or until lightly browned.

Makes 4 servings

Doc's Notes:
Cauliflower is a member of the cruciferous family. Like broccoli, members of this family have been associated with reducing the risk of cancer.

NUTRITIONAL INFORMATION PER SERVING

Calories	96	Saturated Fat (g)	2
Protein (g)	9	Dietary Fiber (g)	3
Carbohydrate (g)	10	Cholesterol (mg)	8
Fat (g)	3	Sodium (mg)	158
Cal. from Fat (%)	25		

Diabetic Exchanges: 1 lean meat, 2 vegetable

PESTO PASTA

This easily prepared pesto tossed with pasta turns a simple dish into a powerhouse of taste. Add some sautéed tomatoes and fresh baby spinach for a real health enhancing Italian dish.

¼ cup blanched almonds
1 cup firmly packed fresh
   basil leaves
4 cloves garlic
3 tablespoons olive oil
3 tablespoons grated
   Parmesan cheese

¼ cup canned fat-free chicken
   broth
Salt and pepper to taste
1 (12-ounce) package angel
   hair pasta

Place the almonds in a food processor and process until finely chopped; set aside. Add the basil and garlic to the food processor until coarsely chopped. Add the oil, cheese, broth, and salt and pepper. Process until finely minced. Add the reserved almonds; process until mixed. Add more broth if needed to thin. Cook the pasta according to package directions; drain and mix with pesto.

Makes 4 to 6 servings

Doc's Notes:
If you do not have almonds, try toasted pecans.

NUTRITIONAL INFORMATION PER SERVING

Calories 326
Protein (g) 10
Carbohydrate (g) 45
Fat (g) 12
Cal. from Fat (%).................. 33

Saturated Fat (g) 2
Dietary Fiber (g) 2
Cholesterol (mg) 3
Sodium (mg) 89

Diabetic Exchanges: 3 starch, 2 fat

SQUASH AND TOMATO CASSEROLE

When squash is in season, this tasty recipe will enhance any dinner. Even if you're not a squash fan, give this recipe a try as it's very good.

2 pounds yellow squash, sliced
1 onion, finely minced
1 teaspoon minced garlic
Salt and pepper to taste

4 slices reduced-fat American cheese
1 (16-ounce) can diced tomatoes, drained, or 1 cup chopped fresh tomatoes

Preheat oven to 350 degrees. In a large skillet coated with nonstick cooking spray, sauté squash, onion, garlic, and salt and pepper, stirring, about 10 minutes or until veggies are tender. Remove from heat, drain excess liquid. Add cheese, stirring until cheese melts. Pour mixture into an 8-inch square casserole. Sprinkle tomatoes over squash. Bake for 20 to 25 minutes.

Makes 6 to 8 servings

Doc's Notes:

The squash and tomatoes make this an excellent source of Vitamin A.

NUTRITIONAL INFORMATION PER SERVING

Calories 60
Protein (g) 5
Carbohydrate (g) 10
Fat (g) 1
Cal. from Fat (%) 14
Saturated Fat (g) 1
Dietary Fiber (g) 3
Cholesterol (mg) 4
Sodium (mg) 237

Diabetic Exchanges: 0.5 lean meat, 2 vegetable

YAM CORNBREAD STUFFING

By adding yams to your traditional stuffing, you add nutrition.

2	cups chopped and peeled raw sweet potatoes (yams)	¼	cup chopped parsley
1	cup chopped onion	1	teaspoon ground ginger
1	cup sliced celery	5	cups crumbled cornbread
2	tablespoons margarine	¼	cup chopped pecans
			Chicken broth

Preheat oven to 375 degrees. In a large skillet, cook sweet potatoes, onion, and celery in margarine for 5 to 7 minutes or until just tender. Spoon mixture into a large mixing bowl. Stir in parsley and ginger. Add cornbread and pecans. Toss gently to coat. Add enough chicken broth to moisten. Place stuffing in a casserole. Bake, uncovered, for 45 minutes or until heated through.

Makes 10 servings

Doc's Notes:

Sweet potatoes are one of the most nutritious foods in the vegetable kingdom. A 5-inch sweet potato contains only about 120 calories.

NUTRITIONAL INFORMATION PER SERVING

Calories	157		
Protein (g)	3	Dietary Fiber (g)	3
Carbohydrate (g)	21	Cholesterol (mg)	12
Fat (g)	7	Sodium (mg)	228
Cal. from Fat (%)	40		
Saturated Fat (g)	1		

Diabetic Exchanges: 1.5 starch,

1 fat

EGGPLANT PARMESAN

A quick and easy version of this popular dish.

2   medium eggplants, peeled
    and cut in ½-inch slices
    (12 slices)
2   onions, sliced into rings
1   (28-ounce) can whole
    peeled tomatoes,
    undrained

1   teaspoon dried oregano
    leaves
½   teaspoon dried basil leaves
Salt and pepper to taste
1   (8-ounce) package part
    skim mozzarella cheese,
    shredded

Preheat oven to 350 degrees. Broil eggplant slices 5 inches from heat, about 5 minutes or until brown on one side. Arrange slices, brown side down, in a 2-quart long casserole dish coated with nonstick cooking spray. Top with onions. In a food processor, combine tomatoes with juice, oregano, basil, and salt and pepper, chopping into small pieces. Pour over eggplant. Bake for 45 minutes. Top with mozzarella cheese and bake an additional 15 minutes.

Makes 4 to 5 servings

Doc's Notes:
Eggplant is very filling, supplying few calories, high in fiber and virtually no fat.

NUTRITIONAL INFORMATION PER SERVING

Calories 230
Protein (g) 16
Carbohydrate (g) 28
Fat (g) 8
Cal. from Fat (%) 29

Saturated Fat (g) 5
Dietary Fiber (g) 9
Cholesterol (mg) 26
Sodium (mg) 455

Diabetic Exchanges: 1.5 lean meat, 6 vegetable

SOUTHWESTERN CHICKEN WITH SALSA

This dish is quick and the homemade salsa baked
with the chicken really adds a fabulous something extra.
For the salsa, I chop my tomatoes in the food processor.

1¾ pounds boneless skinless chicken breasts	Salsa (recipe follows)
2 teaspoons ground cumin	⅔ cup shredded reduced-fat Monterey Jack cheese

Preheat oven to 350 degrees. Coat the chicken breasts on both sides with the cumin. In a large skillet coated with nonstick cooking spray, sauté the breasts over medium heat until brown on both sides. Add salsa and transfer to a baking dish and bake for 20 minutes or until chicken is tender. Sprinkle with the shredded cheese and continue baking until the cheese is melted, about 5 minutes.

Salsa

2 medium tomatoes, chopped	1 tablespoon lime juice
2 tablespoons chopped fresh cilantro	1 teaspoon chopped jalapeño, optional
	⅓ cup chopped onion

Combine the tomato, cilantro, lime juice, jalapeño, and onion in a small bowl.

Makes 6 servings

Doc's Notes:
Add black beans and corn for added fiber and nutrition.

NUTRITIONAL INFORMATION PER SERVING

Calories	197	Saturated Fat (g)	2
Protein (g)	35	Dietary Fiber (g)	1
Carbohydrate (g)	3	Cholesterol (mg)	84
Fat (g)	4	Sodium (mg)	171
Cal. from Fat (%)	20		

Diabetic Exchanges: 4 very lean meat, 1 vegetable

CHICKEN WITH BEAN SAUCE

*Here's a great way to include beans in your meals as
the beans dissolve into the sauce and enhance the flavor.*

2   pounds boneless skinless
    chicken breasts
1   (16-ounce) can fat-free
    refried beans
½   cup chopped red onion
2   (10-ounce) cans diced
    tomatoes and green chiles
    with their juice

1   cup shredded reduced-fat
    sharp Cheddar cheese,
    optional
¼   cup chopped green onions
    (scallions), optional

Preheat oven to 350 degrees. Place chicken breasts in a 2-quart oblong baking dish coated with nonstick cooking spray. Spread the beans to cover the top of the chicken. Sprinkle with the red onion. Pour the tomatoes and juice evenly over the top. Cover with foil and bake 1 hour 20 minutes or until the chicken is done. Sprinkle with the Cheddar cheese and green onions and serve.

Makes 6 servings

Doc's Notes:
Substitute diced tomatoes for a less spicy version. Beans are high in fiber, protein, and carbohydrates.

NUTRITIONAL INFORMATION PER SERVING

Calories 247
Protein (g) 39
Carbohydrate (g) 16
Fat (g) 2
Cal. from Fat (%) 7

Saturated Fat (g) 1
Dietary Fiber (g) 5
Cholesterol (mg) 88
Sodium (mg) 770

Diabetic Exchanges: 5 very lean meat, 1 starch, 1 vegetable

QUICK HERB CHICKEN

I bought a mixed pack of fresh herbs at the grocery and prepared this dish. A mixture of basil, oregano, and rosemary works well. You can always use about 2 teaspoons dry herbs of your choice.

2   tablespoons lemon juice
Black pepper to taste
1   tablespoon minced garlic
2   pounds boneless skinless
      chicken breasts
1   cup all-purpose flour

2   tablespoons olive oil
2   cups canned fat-free
      chicken broth
2   tablespoons Dijon mustard
¼   cup fresh herbs, chopped

In a small bowl, mix the lemon juice, pepper, and garlic together to season the chicken. Dredge each piece of seasoned chicken in flour and place in a heated large skillet coated with nonstick cooking spray and olive oil. Brown chicken on each side. In a small bowl, combine broth, mustard, and herbs; add to chicken in pan. Bring to a boil, lower heat, cover and cook until chicken is tender, about 15 to 20 minutes.

Makes 6 servings

Doc's Notes:
Pasta tossed with olive oil makes a great side dish.

NUTRITIONAL INFORMATION PER SERVING

Calories 298
Protein (g) 38
Carbohydrate (g) 18
Fat (g) 7
Cal. from Fat (%) 21

Saturated Fat (g) 1
Dietary Fiber (g) 1
Cholesterol (mg) 88
Sodium (mg) 426

Diabetic Exchanges: 4 very lean meat, 1 starch, 1 fat

CHICKEN PRIMAVERA

This is one of my all time favorite chicken pasta recipes.
Adjust the onion and garlic to your taste buds.

1 (12-ounce) package
   linguine
1½ pounds boneless skinless
   chicken pieces
¼ cup olive oil
3 cloves garlic, minced
½ pound mushrooms, sliced
1 onion, chopped
1 red bell pepper, cored and
   chopped

½ teaspoon dried oregano
   leaves
½ teaspoon dried basil leaves
½ teaspoon dried thyme
   leaves
Salt and pepper to taste
1 cup frozen peas
¼ cup grated Parmesan
   cheese

Cook linguine according to directions on package; drain. In a large frying pan, cook chicken pieces in olive oil and garlic until lightly browned and done. Watch carefully, tossing to keep from sticking. Add mushrooms, onions, red pepper, and seasonings, sautéing until tender. Add peas, tossing until heated. When pasta is ready, add to chicken mixture, combining well. Add Parmesan cheese and serve.

Makes 6 to 8 servings

Doc's Notes:
A quick recipe that will appeal to the family.

NUTRITIONAL INFORMATION PER SERVING

Calories 360
Protein (g) 29
Carbohydrate (g) 39
Fat (g) 10
Cal. from Fat (%) 24

Saturated Fat (g) 2
Dietary Fiber (g) 3
Cholesterol (mg) 52
Sodium (mg) 139

Diabetic Exchanges: 3 lean meat, 2 starch, 1.5 vegetable

HERBED SHRIMP

A quick recipe to enjoy shrimp. Serve with French bread to dip in the sauce. Try serving with sautéed kale — a cruciferous veggie.

¾ cup Worcestershire sauce
3 tablespoons olive oil
2 tablespoons dried rosemary leaves
3 bay leaves

⅓ cup sherry, optional
2 tablespoons lemon juice
1½ pounds large unpeeled shrimp

In a large bowl, combine all ingredients except shrimp. Add shrimp to mixture and marinate in refrigerator at least 2 to 3 hours. Preheat oven to 400 degrees. Transfer shrimp and marinade to an oblong dish and bake for 20 minutes. Watch closely and turn shrimp.

Makes 4 servings

Doc's Notes:

This is a nice change from red meat. Shrimp are low in fat and calories.

NUTRITIONAL INFORMATION PER SERVING

Calories	234	Saturated Fat (g)	2
Protein (g)	22	Dietary Fiber (g)	1
Carbohydrate (g)	10	Cholesterol (mg)	202
Fat (g)	12	Sodium (mg)	733
Cal. from Fat (%)	45		

Diabetic Exchanges: 3 lean meat, 0.5 other carb., 1.5 fat

SHRIMP, PEPPERS, AND CHEESE GRITS

A nice change is to use grits, which has similar nutritional value to other enriched grains.

1   green bell pepper, cored and sliced
½   cup chopped tomatoes
1½ pounds medium shrimp, peeled
½   cup chopped green onions (scallions)

2   cups canned fat-free chicken broth
1½ cups skim milk
1   cup quick grits
1   cup shredded reduced-fat Cheddar cheese

In a large skillet coated with nonstick cooking spray, sauté the green pepper, tomatoes, and shrimp, cooking until the shrimp are done, about 5 to 7 minutes. Add the green onions, cooking several more minutes. Meanwhile, in a pot, bring the chicken broth and milk to a boil. Stir in the grits. Return to a boil, cover, and reduce to low heat. Cook about 5 minutes or until thickened, stir occasionally. Stir in the cheese. Serve the shrimp over the cheese grits.

Makes 4 to 6 servings

Doc's Notes:
You have to try this to see how delicious it really is. A great source of Vitamin A and fiber, yet low in fat.

NUTRITIONAL INFORMATION PER SERVING

Calories	256	Saturated Fat (g)	3
Protein (g)	25	Dietary Fiber (g)	1
Carbohydrate (g)	27	Cholesterol (mg)	146
Fat (g)	5	Sodium (mg)	516
Cal. from Fat (%)	17		

Diabetic Exchanges: 3 very lean meat, 1.5 starch, 1 vegetable

BAKED TOPPED FISH

Here's a simple way to prepare fresh fish. Remember to include fish in your diet often. Line the pan with foil for easy cleaning.

3 tablespoons light
   mayonnaise
¼ cup chopped green onions
   (scallions), optional
1 tablespoon Worcestershire
   sauce

¼ teaspoon hot pepper sauce
2 pounds trout fillets or fish
   of choice
Salt and pepper to taste
2 tablespoons balsamic
   vinegar

Preheat broiler. In a small bowl, combine the mayonnaise, green onions, Worcestershire sauce, and hot sauce. Lay the fillets in a baking dish. Sprinkle with salt and pepper. Spread with the mayonnaise mixture evenly over the fillets. Drizzle with the vinegar. Place under the broiler for 6 to 10 minutes or until the fish flakes easily with a fork. Watch carefully so it doesn't burn.

Makes 4 servings

Doc's Notes:

Fish is rich in protein, iron, B vitamins, and other nutrients, and can take the place of meats that are high in saturated fat.

NUTRITIONAL INFORMATION PER SERVING

Calories 379
Protein (g) 47
Carbohydrate (g) 3
Fat (g) 19
Cal. from Fat (%) 45

Saturated Fat (g) 3
Dietary Fiber (g) 0
Cholesterol (mg) 133
Sodium (mg) 252

Diabetic Exchanges: 6 lean meat

SALMON PATTIES WITH HORSERADISH CAPER SAUCE

*If you enjoy salmon, this easy recipe will quickly become
a favorite. Perfect when you need a light quick meal.
Serve with Horseradish Caper Sauce, over fresh sautéed
spinach, or on a whole wheat bun for a great sandwich.*

1¼ pounds salmon fillets,
     skinned
⅓ cup finely chopped onion
3   tablespoons light
     mayonnaise

½ teaspoon dried tarragon or
     dill weed
½ cup Italian bread crumbs
Salt and pepper to taste

Trim salmon and cut into 2-inch cubes; place in the food processor or chop finely by hand. Add the onion, mayonnaise, tarragon, and bread crumbs, mixing well. Season to taste. Coat a skillet with nonstick cooking spray and heat. Make the salmon mixture into six patties and brown the patties over a high heat for 1 minute. Lower heat and continue cooking for a few minutes; turn over and continue cooking about 3 more minutes. Do not overcook. Serve with Horseradish Caper Sauce.

Makes 6 patties

Horseradish Caper Sauce
¼ cup light mayonnaise
2   tablespoons prepared
     horseradish
1   tablespoon lemon juice

1   tablespoon finely chopped
     onion
1   teaspoon capers, drained

Stir all ingredients together and refrigerate.

NUTRITIONAL INFORMATION PER SERVING

Calories	212	Saturated Fat (g)	2
Protein (g)	21	Dietary Fiber (g)	1
Carbohydrate (g)	10	Cholesterol (mg)	55
Fat (g)	9	Sodium (mg)	380
Cal. from Fat (%)	40		

Diabetic Exchanges: 3 lean meat, 0.5 starch

SIMPLY SALMON PASTA

An elegant blend of ingredients and flavors.
Salmon contains lots of omega-3 fatty acids, which are
being studied for their many possible healthy benefits.

1	(9-ounce) package spinach tortellini	⅔	cup evaporated skimmed milk
1	(12-ounce) package bow tie pasta	1	cup sugar snap peas
8	ounces salmon filets	½	cup green onions (scallions)
	Salt and pepper to taste	1	teaspoon dried dill weed
¼	teaspoon sugar	⅓	cup grated Parmesan cheese
1	cup canned fat-free chicken broth		

In a large pot of boiling water, add the spinach tortellini and cook for about 10 minutes. To the same pot, add the bow tie pasta and continue cooking until pasta is done. Drain and set aside. Season the salmon with salt and pepper and sugar. In a skillet coated with nonstick cooking spray, cook the salmon, skin side down, over medium-high heat. Turn to other side and cook until done. Remove skin, cut meat into chunks, and set aside. In the same skillet, add chicken broth and evaporated milk. Bring to a boil, reduce heat, and simmer until liquid reduces, about 7 minutes. Add the peas and green onions, cooking several minutes or until peas are crisp tender. Add the cooked pasta, dill, and cheese, tossing carefully. Carefully toss in the salmon.

Makes 6 to 8 servings

NUTRITIONAL INFORMATION PER SERVING

Calories	298	Saturated Fat (g)	2
Protein (g)	18	Dietary Fiber (g)	2
Carbohydrate (g)	43	Cholesterol (mg)	60
Fat (g)	5	Sodium (mg)	269
Cal. from Fat (%)	16		

Diabetic Exchanges: 1 lean meat, 3 starch

HERB BAKED SALMON

A gourmet delight with little or no effort. Spinach
or Swiss chard makes a nice nutritional side.

2 pounds salmon fillets	¼ teaspoon dried thyme leaves
1 tablespoon margarine, melted	½ teaspoon minced garlic
Salt and pepper to taste	¼ teaspoon dried marjoram, optional
1 tablespoon finely chopped parsley	¼ teaspoon dried rosemary
¼ cup Dijon honey mustard	1 tablespoon lemon juice

Preheat oven to 350 degrees. Place salmon fillets in an oblong baking dish coated with nonstick cooking spray. In a bowl combine melted margarine, salt and pepper, parsley, mustard, thyme, garlic, marjoram, rosemary, and lemon juice. Pour mixture over salmon. Cover with foil. Bake for 30 to 35 minutes or grill if desired. Serve with veggies.

Makes 6 servings

Doc's Notes:
Salmon contains omega 3 fatty acids. Omega 3's have anti-clotting properties and may be protective against heart attacks and perhaps high blood pressure.

NUTRITIONAL INFORMATION PER SERVING

Calories	214	Saturated Fat (g)	1
Protein (g)	30	Dietary Fiber (g)	0
Carbohydrate (g)	4	Cholesterol (mg)	79
Fat (g)	7	Sodium (mg)	134
Cal. from Fat (%)	32		

Diabetic Exchanges: 4 lean meat

TUNA STEAKS WITH HORSERADISH SAUCE

Marinate the steaks, cook, and serve with this incredible sauce for an effortless, outstanding meal. "The easy gourmet!" The tuna may also be grilled or cooked inside on a grill skillet. Tuna is high in protein and low in fat.

4	(6- to 8-ounce) tuna steaks	½	tablespoon prepared
½	cup teriyaki sauce		horseradish
½	cup fat-free Italian dressing	1	tablespoon Dijon mustard
½	cup nonfat plain yogurt		

Rinse the tuna steaks and pat dry. In a flat dish, combine the teriyaki sauce and Italian dressing with the tuna. Cover and refrigerate for at least 2 hours. Heat a skillet coated with nonstick cooking spray over medium heat until hot. Cook the tuna about 3 to 5 minutes on each side, depending on thickness, until done. In a small bowl, mix together the sour cream, horseradish, and mustard. Top each steak with a dollop of sauce before serving.

Makes 4 servings

Doc's Notes:
Tuna is a fish rich in omega 3 fatty acids.

NUTRITIONAL INFORMATION PER SERVING

Calories	218	Saturated Fat (g)	1
Protein (g)	42	Dietary Fiber (g)	0
Carbohydrate (g)	5	Cholesterol (mg)	77
Fat (g)	2	Sodium (mg)	595
Cal. from Fat (%)	8		

Diabetic Exchanges: 5 very lean meat, 0.5 other carb.

LOADED ENCHILADAS

Sometimes ground beef just hits the spot. These are great for a family and also freeze well! This simple recipe is loaded with great ingredients that will give enchiladas a good name. For chicken enchiladas, substitute chicken for the ground beef and include some salsa and cheese when filling the enchiladas. Sprinkle with green onions.

1½ pounds ground sirloin	Salt and pepper to taste
1 small onion, chopped	16 flour tortillas
½ teaspoon minced garlic	2 (14-ounce) cans enchilada
1 tablespoon chili powder	sauce
1 teaspoon ground cumin	1½ cups shredded reduced-fat
1 cup canned Mexican-style	sharp Cheddar cheese
corn, drained	1 cup chopped tomato
1 (15-ounce) can black or	
kidney beans, drained and	
rinsed	

Preheat oven to 350 degrees. In a skillet, cook beef, onion, and garlic until done. Drain any excess grease. Stir in the chili powder, cumin, corn, beans, and salt and pepper, mixing well. Divide the mixture among the tortillas, roll up, and place in a 2-quart oblong casserole dish coated with nonstick cooking spray. Pour the enchilada sauce on top. Sprinkle with cheese and tomato. Bake for 15 minutes or until thoroughly heated and cheese is melted.

Makes 16 enchiladas

NUTRITIONAL INFORMATION PER SERVING

Calories	325	Saturated Fat (g)	4
Protein (g)	18	Dietary Fiber (g)	5
Carbohydrate (g)	39	Cholesterol (mg)	21
Fat (g)	10	Sodium (mg)	871
Cal. from Fat (%)	27		

Diabetic Exchanges: 1.5 lean meat, 2 starch, 2 vegetable

MEATY CABBAGE CASSEROLE

This recipe is a quick and easy alternative to individually stuffing all those cabbage leaves; yet has the same appeal.

1½	pounds ground sirloin	1	(¾-pound) head of cabbage, coarsely shredded
1	onion chopped		
1	teaspoon minced garlic	1	(27-ounce) jar spaghetti sauce
¼	teaspoon black pepper		
3	cups cooked white or brown rice	¼	cup light brown sugar
		1	cup shredded reduced-fat Cheddar cheese

Preheat oven to 350 degrees. In a large skillet, cook the beef, onion, and garlic until the beef is done. Drain any excess grease. Add the pepper and cooked rice, mixing well. Spoon the meat mixture into a 3-quart casserole dish coated with nonstick cooking spray. Top with the shredded cabbage. In a bowl, mix together the spaghetti sauce and brown sugar. Pour the sauce over the cabbage. Bake, covered, for 1 hour, 15 minutes, or until the cabbage is tender. Sprinkle with the Cheddar cheese and continue baking for 5 minutes, or until the cheese is melted.

Makes 6 to 8 servings

Doc's Notes:

Cabbage is a cruciferous vegetable which has been identified as possibly being protective against cancer.

NUTRITIONAL INFORMATION PER SERVING

Calories	366	Saturated Fat (g)	5
Protein (g)	25	Dietary Fiber (g)	3
Carbohydrate (g)	38	Cholesterol (mg)	39
Fat (g)	12	Sodium (mg)	619
Cal. from Fat (%)	30		

Diabetic Exchanges: 3 lean meat, 1 starch, 3 vegetable, 0.5 other carb.

ITALIAN-STYLE POT ROAST

This well-flavored recipe can also be made in a slow cooker. Everyone loves a pot roast and gravy. Serve this with rice or potatoes.

1 (4- to 5-pound) beef round roast
2 cups canned beef broth
½ cup Burgundy wine, optional
3 tablespoons no-salt-added tomato paste
1 (28-ounce) can no-salt-added whole tomatoes, chopped, with their juice
2 cloves garlic, pressed
1 tablespoon dried basil leaves

1 tablespoon dried oregano leaves
2 bay leaves
1 pound carrots, cut into 1-inch pieces
3 onions quartered
1 pound fresh mushrooms, halved
1 tablespoon margarine
2 tablespoons all-purpose flour

Preheat oven to 350 degrees. Place the roast in a large pot. Pour in the beef broth and wine. Add the tomato paste and stir. Add the tomatoes with their juice. Blend in the garlic, basil, oregano, and bay leaves. Cover and cook in the oven for 1½ hours. Add the carrots, onions, and mushrooms. Cover and continue cooking for 1½ hours or until the meat is tender. Transfer the meat to a carving board. Mash the margarine and flour together to form a paste. Place the pot over medium high heat and bring the liquid to a boil. Whisk in the paste to thicken the sauce. Serve meat with the vegetables and the sauce. Discard bay leaves.

Makes 8 to 10 servings

NUTRITIONAL INFORMATION PER SERVING

Calories	399	Saturated Fat (g)	4
Protein (g)	54	Dietary Fiber (g)	4
Carbohydrate (g)	17	Cholesterol (mg)	123
Fat (g)	11	Sodium (mg)	366
Cal. from Fat (%)	26		

Diabetic Exchanges: 6 lean meat, 3 vegetable

GRILLED PORK TENDERLOIN

Pork tenderloins are very lean and a great alternative to chicken or beef. Keep tenderloins in your freezer to defrost for a quick dinner.

1	teaspoon olive oil	1	teaspoon Dijon mustard
¼	cup balsamic vinegar	1	teaspoon dried rosemary
1	tablespoon honey	2	(1-pound) pork tenderloins

In a small bowl, combine the olive oil, balsamic vinegar, honey, Dijon mustard, and rosemary. Trim the fat from the tenderloins. Place tenderloins in a dish and pour the marinade over them. Refrigerate for 2 hours or longer. Preheat oven to 350 degrees. Place the tenderloins on a rack in a roasting pan coated with nonstick cooking spray. Bake for 50 minutes to 1 hour or until a meat thermometer registers 160 degrees. Baste frequently with the marinade and discard any remaining after cooking.

Makes 6 servings

NUTRITIONAL INFORMATION PER SERVING

Calories	200	Saturated Fat (g)	2
Protein (g)	32	Dietary Fiber (g)	0
Carbohydrate (g)	3	Cholesterol (mg)	90
Fat (g)	6	Sodium (mg)	75
Cal. from Fat (%)	28		

Diabetic Exchanges: 4 lean meat

SAVORY LAMB CHOPS

Rich in flavor, these chops will please any palate. I even use this marinade with veal and beef. Serve with veggies and a baked sweet potato for a complete meal.

1 cup canned beef broth
3 tablespoons orange marmalade
3 tablespoons balsamic vinegar
¼ cup chopped onion
1 tablespoon dried marjoram

1 tablespoon dried rosemary leaves
1 tablespoon minced garlic
2 pounds lamb loin chops (1-inch thick), excess fat trimmed

In a shallow dish, combine beef broth, marmalade, vinegar, onion, marjoram, rosemary, and garlic. Pour the marinade over lamb chops. Cover and marinate in refrigerator 8 hours or overnight, turning occasionally. Preheat grill to medium or turn on broiler. Grill or broil lamb 8 to 15 minutes on each side or to desired doneness, basting with reserved marinade. Discard any leftover marinade.

Makes 6 to 8 servings

Doc's Notes:

Lamb is leaner than most cuts of beef. It is an excellent source of protein, iron, zinc, and Vitamin B12.

NUTRITIONAL INFORMATION PER SERVING

Calories 123
Protein (g) 15
Carbohydrate (g) 3
Fat (g) 5
Cal. from Fat (%) 37

Saturated Fat (g) 2
Dietary Fiber (g) 0
Cholesterol (mg) 48
Sodium (mg) 108

Diabetic Exchanges: 2 lean meat

ITALIAN VEAL SUPREME

Veal and pasta are a natural together, and with the spices and olives, this dish has a distinct personality. There is not a lot of sauce in this dish but there is a lot of flavor.

1 (12-ounce) package angel hair pasta
1 large onion, thinly sliced
1 pound thinly sliced veal (scaloppini), cut into 1-inch strips
2 tablespoons all-purpose flour
½ cup dry white wine or chicken broth
1 teaspoon minced garlic

Salt and pepper to taste
1 teaspoon dried oregano leaves
1 teaspoon dried thyme leaves
5 medium plum (Roma) tomatoes, cut into wedges
1 (2¼-ounce) can sliced ripe black olives, drained
2 tablespoons chopped parsley

Cook the pasta according to package directions; drain and set aside. In a large skillet coated with nonstick cooking spray, over medium heat, sauté the onion until tender, about 5 minutes. Sprinkle the veal with the flour and add the veal to the skillet, stirring constantly, cooking the veal until lightly browned. Stir in the wine, garlic, salt and pepper, oregano, and thyme. Bring to a boil; cover, reduce the heat, and simmer 8 to 10 minutes or until the veal is almost tender. Add the tomatoes and olives; cover and simmer 5 minutes or until thoroughly heated. Serve the veal mixture over the pasta; sprinkle with parsley.

Makes 6 servings

NUTRITIONAL INFORMATION PER SERVING

Calories 354	Saturated Fat (g) 1
Protein (g) 25	Dietary Fiber (g) 3
Carbohydrate (g) 51	Cholesterol (mg) 59
Fat (g) 4	Sodium (mg) 153
Cal. from Fat (%) 9	

Diabetic Exchanges: 2 very lean meat, 3 starch, 1 vegetable

ALMOST BETTER THAN SEX CAKE

The name says it all when you have a sweet tooth and this is such an easy recipe. Keep ingredients in pantry to prepare anytime.

1   (18¼-ounce) box reduced-fat yellow cake mix
½   cup skim milk
¼   cup water
⅓   cup canola oil
2   large eggs
2   large egg whites
1   cup nonfat plain yogurt
1   (4-serving) box instant vanilla pudding
1   (4-ounce) bar German chocolate, grated
⅓   cup semi-sweet chocolate chips
⅓   cup chopped pecans

Preheat oven to 350 degrees. Combine all ingredients except chocolate chips and pecans in a large mixing bowl. Beat slightly, only until mixture is combined. Stir in chocolate chips and pecans. Pour batter into a 10-inch fluted Bundt pan coated with nonstick cooking spray and dusted with flour. Bake for 50 to 55 minutes. Do not overbake.

Makes 20 servings

Doc's Notes:
Chocolate is an antioxidant!

NUTRITIONAL INFORMATION PER SERVING

Calories	229	Saturated Fat (g)	3
Protein (g)	4	Dietary Fiber (g)	1
Carbohydrate (g)	32	Cholesterol (mg)	24
Fat (g)	11	Sodium (mg)	269
Cal. from Fat (%)	40		

Diabetic Exchanges: 2 other carb., 2 fat

BANANA CAKE WITH CREAM CHEESE ICING

Try using 1½ cups whole wheat flour and 1 cup all-purpose flour.
For a variation add ½ cup mini chocolate chips or golden raisins.
When you have ripe bananas, it's time for this cake.

2½ cups all-purpose flour	1 cup dark brown sugar
1 teaspoon baking powder	2 large eggs
1½ teaspoons baking soda	1½ cups mashed bananas
1 teaspoon ground cinnamon	2 teaspoons vanilla extract
¼ cup canola oil	1 cup buttermilk

Preheat oven to 350 degrees. In a bowl, combine flour, baking powder, baking soda, and cinnamon; set aside. In a mixing bowl, beat oil and brown sugar until light. Add eggs, mixing well. Add bananas and vanilla. Add dry ingredients alternately with buttermilk. Pour batter evenly into three 9-inch round baking pans coated with nonstick cooking spray. Bake for 20 minutes or until a toothpick inserted comes out clean. Cool and ice.

Cream Cheese Icing

1 (8-ounce) package light cream cheese, softened	1 (16-ounce) box confectioners' sugar
3 tablespoons margarine, softened	1 teaspoon vanilla extract

In a mixing bowl, beat the cream cheese and margarine until smooth. Add the confectioners' sugar and beat until light. Blend in the vanilla. When cake is cool, ice with Cream Cheese Icing.

Makes 16 servings

NUTRITIONAL INFORMATION PER SERVING

Calories	351	Saturated Fat (g)	3
Protein (g)	5	Dietary Fiber (g)	1
Carbohydrate (g)	63	Cholesterol (mg)	34
Fat (g)	9	Sodium (mg)	270
Cal. from Fat (%)	22		

Diabetic Exchanges: 1 starch, 0.5 fruit, 3 other carb., 1.5 fat

YAM CAKE WITH CRANBERRY CREAM CHEESE FILLING

Satisfy your sweet tooth with this easy, spicy yam cake that starts with a cake mix. Yams and cranberries add nutrition.

1 (18¼-ounce) box reduced-fat yellow cake mix
1 teaspoon ground cinnamon
½ teaspoon ground nutmeg
3 large eggs
2 tablespoons canola oil
1⅓ cups water
1 (15-ounce) can sweet potatoes (yams), drained and mashed (1 cup)
1 cup drained crushed pineapple
1 teaspoon vanilla extract

Preheat oven to 350 degrees. Coat three 9-inch round cake pans with nonstick cooking spray. In a large mixing bowl, combine the cake mix, cinnamon, nutmeg, eggs, oil, water, sweet potatoes, crushed pineapple, and vanilla, mixing at low speed until well combined. Pour into prepared pans. Bake for 20 to 25 minutes or until wooden pick inserted comes out clean.

Cranberry Cream Cheese Icing

1 (8-ounce) package light cream cheese
3 tablespoons margarine
1 (16-ounce) box confectioners' sugar
1 teaspoon vanilla extract
½ cup dried cranberries

In mixing bowl, beat together cream cheese and margarine until creamy. Gradually add confectioners' sugar, mixing until smooth. Add vanilla, mixing well. Remove ⅔ cup icing and mix with cranberries. Use cranberry mixture to ice between layers and ice sides and top of cake with remaining icing.

Makes 16 to 20 servings

Doc's Notes:
The pineapple is a good source of Vitamin C. This cake is a good source of beta carotene and Vitamins C and B.

NUTRITIONAL INFORMATION PER SERVING

Calories	292	Saturated Fat (g)	3
Protein (g)	4	Dietary Fiber (g)	1
Carbohydrate (g)	51	Cholesterol (mg)	39
Fat (g)	8	Sodium (mg)	260
Cal. from Fat (%)	25		

Diabetic Exchanges: 0.5 fruit, 3 other carb., 1.5 fat

STRAWBERRY ANGEL FOOD CAKE

Great during strawberry season as it's so light and so quick!
Buy an angel food cake at the grocery or you can prepare a mix.

1   (16-ounce) commercially
      prepared angel food cake
1   (8-ounce) package light
      cream cheese, softened

½   cup sugar
¼   cup evaporated skimmed
      milk
2   pints strawberries, hulled
      and sliced

Use a serrated knife to slice the angel food cake horizontally into 3 equal layers. Prepare the filling by creaming together the cream cheese, sugar, and evaporated skimmed milk. Top the bottom cake layer with the filling and strawberries. Repeat the layers. Refrigerate.

Makes 10 to 12 slices

NUTRITIONAL INFORMATION PER SERVING

Calories	190	Saturated Fat (g)	2
Protein (g)	5	Dietary Fiber (g)	2
Carbohydrate (g)	35	Cholesterol (mg)	9
Fat (g)	3	Sodium (mg)	378
Cal. from Fat (%)	16		

Diabetic Exchanges: 0.5 fruit, 2 other carb., 0.5 fat

PEANUT BUTTER-BANANA PIE

Firm bananas rather than extra-ripe ones work best in this pie.

1¼ cups reduced-fat vanilla wafer crumbs (about 30 cookies)

2 tablespoons margarine, melted

⅔ cup sugar

3 tablespoons cornstarch

1½ cups skim milk

2 large eggs, lightly beaten

2 tablespoons reduced-fat crunchy peanut butter

1 teaspoon vanilla extract

3 cups sliced banana

1½ cups frozen fat-free whipped topping, thawed

In a small bowl, mix together the vanilla wafer crumbs and margarine. Press into a 9-inch pie plate; set aside. Combine sugar and cornstarch in a small heavy saucepan. Gradually add milk, stirring with a whisk until well-blended. Cook over medium heat until mixture comes to a boil. Cook for 1 minute, stirring with a whisk. Gradually add about ⅓ cup hot custard to beaten eggs, stirring constantly with a whisk. Return egg mixture to saucepan. Cook over medium heat, stirring constantly, for about 1 minute or until thick. Remove from heat and stir in peanut butter and vanilla. Cool slightly. Arrange banana slices in bottom of prepared crust; spoon filling over bananas. Press plastic wrap onto the surface of filling; refrigerate until well chilled. Remove plastic wrap. Spread whipped topping evenly over filling. Refrigerate.

Makes 8 servings

Doc's Notes:

Bananas are a great source of potassium, while peanut butter is a great source of protein, iron, magnesium, and fiber. Potassium is vital for muscle contraction, nerve impulses, and proper function of the heart and kidneys.

NUTRITIONAL INFORMATION PER SERVING

Calories	288	Saturated Fat (g)	1
Protein (g)	5	Dietary Fiber (g)	2
Carbohydrate (g)	52	Cholesterol (mg)	54
Fat (g)	7	Sodium (mg)	153
Cal. from Fat (%)	21		

Diabetic Exchanges: 0.5 starch, 1 fruit, 2 other carb., 1 fat

AMBROSIA CRUMBLE

For this recipe, I suggest using fresh fruit, and for a real treat, serve over frozen vanilla yogurt. This is one of those desserts I attack right when it comes out of the oven.

1 cup all-purpose flour
½ cup light brown sugar
3 tablespoons margarine
¼ cup flaked coconut
2 cups fresh pineapple chunks

3 large navel oranges, peeled and sectioned
3 large bananas, cut into ½-inch thick slices
2 tablespoons lemon juice
1 teaspoon coconut extract

Preheat oven to 350 degrees. In a bowl, combine the flour and brown sugar; cut in the margarine with a pastry blender or fork until the mixture is crumbly. Set aside. In a bowl, combine the coconut, pineapple, oranges, bananas, lemon juice, and coconut extract; toss well. Place the fruit mixture in a 13x9x2-inch baking dish coated with nonstick cooking spray. Sprinkle with the reserved flour mixture. Bake, uncovered, for 45 minutes, until golden.

Makes 10 servings

Doc's Notes:
Excellent source of Vitamin C and potassium.

NUTRITIONAL INFORMATION PER SERVING

Calories	206	Saturated Fat (g)	2
Protein (g)	3	Dietary Fiber (g)	3
Carbohydrate (g)	40	Cholesterol (mg)	0
Fat (g)	5	Sodium (mg)	55
Cal. from Fat (%)	20		

Diabetic Exchanges: 0.5 starch, 1 fruit, 1 other carb., 1 fat

C

Index

Index

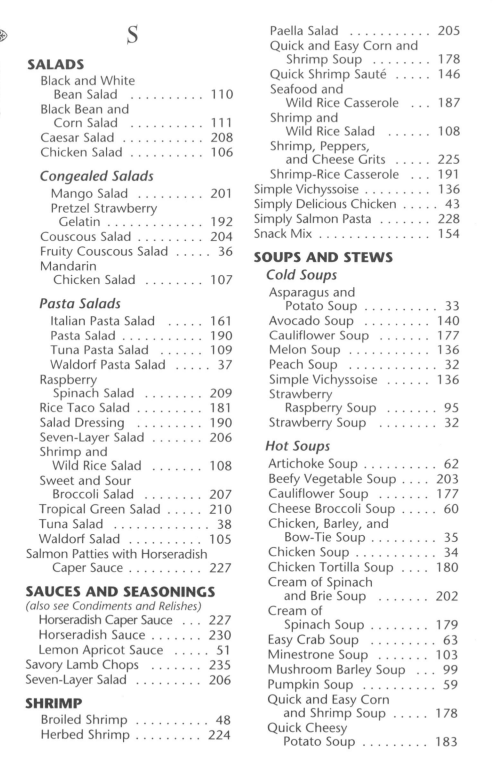

S

Index

HOLLY B. CLEGG

13431 Woodmont Court
Baton Rouge, Louisiana 70810-5334
1-800-88HOLLY

Please send me the following copies:

Eating Well Through Cancer:
   Easy Recipes & Recommendations
   During & After Treatment   _____ copies @ $21.95 = _____

The Holly Clegg Trim &
   Terrific™ Cookbook   _____ copies @ $24.95 = _____
   More Than 500 Fast, Easy, and
   Healthy Recipes

Holly Clegg Trim &
   Terrific™ Home Entertaining _____ copies @ $19.95 = _____

SUBTOTAL $ _____

(Louisiana residents add 8.9% sales tax) TAX $ _____

POSTAGE AND HANDLING ($4.00) $ _____

(Postage and handling for each additional book $1.00) $ _____

TOTAL $ _____

Name_____

Address_____

City_____ State _____ Zip Code_____

Telephone Number (____)_____

Please charge to my   ☐ MasterCard   ☐ VISA

Card #_____ Expiration Date_____

Signature of Cardholder_____

OR CHARGE BY PHONE 1-800-88HOLLY

Make Checks payable to Holly B. Clegg, Inc.

Visit My Website: www.hollyclegg.com